CREATIVE
HOMEOWNER®

trim
step-by-step

CREATIVE HOMEOWNER®, Upper Saddle River, New Jersey

COPYRIGHT © 2003, 2009

CRE🏠TIVE
HOMEOWNER®

A Division of Federal Marketing Corp.
Upper Saddle River, NJ

SMART GUIDE: TRIM

AUTHOR	Neal Barrett
GRAPHIC DESIGNER	Kathryn Wityk
MANAGING EDITOR	Fran Donegan
JUNIOR EDITOR	Jennifer Calvert
TECHNICAL EDITOR	Steve Willson
PHOTO COORDINATOR	Mary Dolan
DIGITAL IMAGING SPECIALIST	Frank Dyer
INDEXER	Schroeder Indexing Services
SMART GUIDE® SERIES COVER DESIGN	Clarke Barre
FRONT COVER PHOTOGRAPHY	Neal Barrett

CREATIVE HOMEOWNER

VICE PRESIDENT AND PUBLISHER	Timothy O. Bakke
MANAGING EDITOR	Fran J. Donegan
ART DIRECTOR	David Geer
PRODUCTION COORDINATOR	Sara M. Markowitz

Current Printing (last digit)
10 9 8 7 6 5 4 3 2 1

Manufactured in the United States of America

Smart Guide: Trim, Second Edition
Library of Congress Control Number: 2008936183
ISBN-10: 1-58011-445-8
ISBN-13: 978-1-58011-445-5

CREATIVE HOMEOWNER®
A Division of Federal Marketing Corp.
24 Park Way
Upper Saddle River, NJ 07458
www.creativehomeowner.com

Metric Conversion

Length

1 inch	25.4 mm
1 foot	0.3048 m
1 yard	0.9144 m
1 mile	1.61 km

Area

1 square inch	645 mm²
1 square foot	0.0929 m²
1 square yard	0.8361 m²
1 acre	4046.86 m²
1 square mile	2.59 km²

Volume

1 cubic inch	16.3870 cm³
1 cubic foot	0.03 m³
1 cubic yard	0.77 m³

Common Lumber Equivalents

Sizes: Metric cross sections are so close to their U.S. sizes, as noted below, that for most purposes they may be considered equivalents.

Dimensional lumber	1 x 2	19 x 38 mm
	1 x 4	19 x 89 mm
	2 x 2	38 x 38 mm
	2 x 4	38 x 89 mm
	2 x 6	38 x 140 mm
	2 x 8	38 x 184 mm
	2 x 10	38 x 235 mm
	2 x 12	38 x 286 mm
Sheet sizes	4 x 8 ft.	1200 x 2400 mm
	4 x 10 ft.	1200 x 3000 mm
Sheet thicknesses	¼ in.	6 mm
	⅜ in.	9 mm
	½ in.	12 mm
	¾ in.	19 mm
Stud/joist spacing	16 in. o.c.	400 mm o.c.
	24 in. o.c.	600 mm o.c.

Capacity

1 fluid ounce	29.57 mL
1 pint	473.18 mL
1 quart	1.14 L
1 gallon	3.79 L

Weight

1 ounce	28.35g
1 pound	0.45kg

Temperature

Celsius = Fahrenheit – 32 x ⁵⁄₉
Fahrenheit = Celsius x 1.8 + 32

Nail Size & Length

Penny Size	Nail Length
2d	1"
3d	1¼ in.
4d	1½ in.
5d	1¾ in.
6d	2 in.
7d	2¼ in.
8d	2½ in.
9d	2¾ in.
10d	3"
12d	3¼ in.
16d	3½ in.

contents

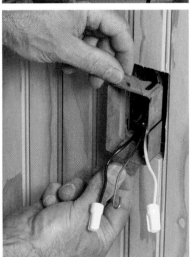

safety first

Though all the designs and methods in this book have been reviewed for safety, it is not possible to overstate the importance of using the safest construction methods possible. What follows are reminders; some do's and don'ts of basic carpentry. They are not substitutes for your own common sense.

■ *Always* use caution, care, and good judgment when following the procedures described in this book.

■ *Always* be sure that the electrical setup is safe; be sure that no circuit is overloaded and that all power tools and electrical outlets are properly grounded. Do not use power tools in wet locations.

■ *Always* read container labels on paints, solvents, and other products; provide ventilation, and observe all other warnings.

■ *Always* read the manufacturer's instructions for using a tool, especially the warnings.

■ *Always* use hold-downs and push sticks whenever possible when working on a table saw. Avoid working short pieces if you can.

■ *Always* remove the key from any drill chuck (portable or press) before starting the drill.

■ *Always* pay deliberate attention to how a tool works so that you can avoid being injured.

■ *Always* know the limitations of your tools. Do not try to force them to do what they were not designed to do.

■ *Always* make sure that any adjustment is locked before proceeding. For example, always check the rip fence on a table saw or the bevel adjustment on a portable saw before starting to work.

■ *Always* clamp small pieces firmly to a bench or other work surface when using a power tool on them.

■ *Always* wear the appropriate rubber or work gloves when handling chemicals, moving or stacking lumber, or doing heavy construction.

■ *Always* wear a disposable face mask when you create dust by sawing or sanding. Use a special filtering respirator when working with toxic substances and solvents.

■ *Always* wear eye protection, especially when using power tools or striking metal on metal or concrete; a chip can fly off, for example, when chiseling concrete.

■ *Always* be aware that there is seldom enough time for your body's reflexes to save you from injury from a power tool in a dangerous situation; everything happens too fast. Be *alert!*

■ *Always* keep your hands away from the business ends of blades, cutters, and bits.

■ *Always* hold a circular saw firmly, usually with both hands so that you know where they are.

■ *Always* use a drill with an auxiliary handle to control the torque when large-size bits are used.

■ *Always* check your local building codes when planning new construction. The codes are intended to protect public safety and should be observed to the letter.

■ *Never* work with power tools when you are tired or under the influence of alcohol or drugs.

■ *Never* cut tiny pieces of wood or pipe using a power saw. Cut small pieces off larger pieces.

■ *Never* change a saw blade or a drill or router bit unless the power cord is unplugged. Do not depend on the switch being off; you might accidentally hit it.

■ *Never* work in insufficient lighting.

■ *Never* work while wearing loose clothing, hanging hair, open cuffs, or jewelry.

■ *Never* work with dull tools. Have them sharpened, or learn how to sharpen them yourself.

■ *Never* use a power tool on a workpiece—large or small—that is not firmly supported.

■ *Never* saw a workpiece that spans a large distance between horses without close support on each side of the cut; the piece can bend, closing on and jamming the blade, causing saw kickback.

■ *Never* support a workpiece from underneath with your leg or other part of your body when sawing.

■ *Never* carry sharp or pointed tools, such as utility knives, awls, or chisels, in your pocket. If you want to carry such tools, use a special-purpose tool belt with leather pockets and holders.

Trimwork in the Home

In many ways, our homes tell the story of who we are and the things we cherish. We fill the rooms with objects that comfort us, promote our sense of well-being, and sometimes stimulate our intellect. The colors and furnishings of a home are a large part of that story. But the blank canvas for these trimmings is the building itself. The layout of the rooms, the number and size of windows and doors, and the height of the ceiling form the foundation for all that we bring to the task of transforming a house into a home.

Adding Style. Beyond the basic structure, a prime contributor to the style of any home is the architectural trim or woodwork: the casing, baseboard, paneling, and assorted moldings that mark the transitions between surfaces and define room openings. Some of these elements serve practical functions—such as covering the spaces between wallboard and floor or ensuring that doors operate properly—and some are purely decorative. But each of these trim components contributes to the architectural spirit of a home. The shape of each profile and its relation to the adjoining surfaces and the room as a whole make a statement about style. The nature of trim invites our eyes to move in deliberate ways. It uses the traditional architectural devices of dimension, line, proportion, and shadow to create a mood.

Trim Designs. Although trim is definitely part of the structure of a home, it is by no means sacred. In a bow to cost savings, many newer homes are constructed with the simplest possible molding profiles and without any embellishments beyond the basic functional necessities—baseboard and casing. While there is certainly nothing wrong with this approach, more elaborate treatments can dramatically change the feel of one room or an entire home. In these pages you will find a step-by-step guide to many design options and techniques for replacing existing trim or tackling new trim in a remodeling project or addition. You can transform your home, and add value—and experience the satisfaction of knowing that you did it yourself.

Ceiling beams add a distinctive touch to this traditional home.

Arts-and-crafts themes contribute to the design of this wall treatment.

Trim Elements

The basic types of trim and molding found in the average home are fairly simple, but there is an almost endless variety of molding profiles from which to choose. The trick is to understand what is available and what looks best in your home. Once you understand the elements of interior woodwork, you can decide to follow a traditional design theme or create a more individual look by mixing features of separate styles.

The arched entry shown above is trimmed with bright-white casing that frames the colorful room setting as well as the artwork hanging on the far wall.

Homes built in the first half of the century, right, tend to have distinctive trimwork, especially around mantels, windows, and cornices.

Types of Trim

Beginning at the junction of the floor and wall, base trim is used to cover the gap between the discrete materials used for each surface. Modern homes typically use a one-piece *baseboard* that is 3 to 4½ inches high. A small *shoe molding* is often nailed to the baseboard to cover any gap between the baseboard and the floor. Earlier, traditional styles featured taller and more elaborate treatments. These often combined three or four separate molding profiles to create a stronger visual line at the bottom of the walls.

Casing. The sides and tops of window and door openings are lined with wooden members called *jambs*, and the gaps between the jambs and the wall treatment are covered by trimwork or molding called *casing*. In applications where moving parts are involved, the casing acts to lock the jambs in place, maintaining an even gap around the

window or door, and ensuring reliable operation.

In some homes, windows are trimmed with casing on sides, top, and bottom in what is called a picture-frame style. But in a more traditional treatment, the bottom of a window is provided with a *stool*, a shelf-like horizontal piece that extends across the opening. Under the stool, another piece of molding, called an *apron*, covers the gap between the stool and wall surface. In many cases, the apron is cut from the same molding profile used for the window casing.

Cornice Molding. *Crown* or *cornice molding* is applied at the joint between the walls and ceiling. These treatments can be simple one-piece moldings or elaborate constructions with layers of different profiles. Often a cornice will sit atop a *frieze*, or horizontal band, located near the top of the wall surface.

The molding profile of the casing shown left works well with the bright color scheme of the room.

Choose cornice and casing profiles, top, that complement one another.

Distinctive moldings, below, add texture and visual interest to a monochromatic color scheme.

Wall Treatments. Originally conceived to protect wall surfaces from damage by chair backs, a *chair rail* can be a single or compound molding. Although there are some profiles that are sold specifically as chair rail molding, other shapes are often used alone or in combination for this purpose. So the design possibilities are endless. When *wainscoting,* or wall paneling, is applied to the lower portion of a wall, the molding that acts as a cap can sometimes be considered a chair rail.

If the wainscot cap is designed as a narrow shelf with grooved top surface, it is called a plate rail and can be used to display decorative china or artwork. Sometimes a plate rail is used alone, without a wainscot being applied.

Sometimes moldings are applied directly to a wall surface in square, rectangular, or even parallelogram shapes. These are called *wall frames.* They can be fashioned from either specifically named panel molding or other profiles. Wall frames are strictly ornamental elements. For a truly dramatic presentation, combine a series of wall frames with decorative painting techniques or wallpaper treatments.

Ceiling Treatments. Ceilings can be adorned with beams or coffers. In a *beamed ceiling,* either solid structural timbers are left exposed or built-up beams are mounted to the ceiling in a parallel row. Often the beams are trimmed with decorative molding. If the beams run in two directions and form recessed panels, these panels are called *coffers.* Although coffers were originally a detail cast in plaster, it is also possible to use plain or figured wooden surfaces for these panels. Most often, coffered ceilings include some type of molding at the junction of the beam and coffer surfaces.

Columns and Pilasters. Transitions between rooms are frequently a focal point for decorative trim. Round or square *columns* can be mounted on decorative bases or platforms in an archway. *Pilasters* are rectangular, projecting moldings mounted vertically to the wall. These are treated in the same way as a column, with trimmed base and capital, and can be used to bracket room openings or architectural features like a niche, fireplace, or built-in shelving unit.

Chair rail and wall frames, opposite, set a traditional tone for this room.

An unusual ceiling, right, calls for an imaginative ceiling trim design.

Interior columns, below left, may not be structural, but they should appear to be.

Pilasters, below right, add a classical touch to the design.

trim materials

Lumber for Trimwork

If you stroll down the lumber aisles at the local home center, you will see racks of interior moldings and boards in pine, red oak, and poplar. These species are the most common choices for interior millwork, and most stock molding profiles are available in these woods. Millwork is the term used to describe lumber that has been machined into particular profiles. This can include flat stock for door jambs, as well as intricate molding.

Pine

Pine has long been the default choice for interior millwork for a number of reasons. Because pine trees grow faster than many other species, manufacturers have a source of lumber that can be renewed, keeping the cost of materials more manageable. Door and window manufacturers have used pine because of its high resin content, which makes it more resistant to rot than some other species. Builders like pine because it is relatively lightweight, it is easy to install, and it takes a nice finish.

Lumber Grades. Most interior trim jobs use a combination of molded stock and flat lumber. When you shop for pine lumber, you will find that it is available in either clear or common grades. While the details of lumber grading can get somewhat technical, a functional approach is simple. Clear, or select, grades have relatively few defects such as knots or pitch pockets, while common-grade lumber can include more of these defects. The difference in price in these material grades can be substantial, but for most trim work you should choose clear, or select, stock. The reasons for using clear grades have more to do with just the appearance of the job. The additional labor involved in cutting around defects, and the inevitable waste, makes the efficient use of lesser grades questionable, even for a painted finish. And knots that are left in place will usually become visible after a time, even through a first-quality paint job.

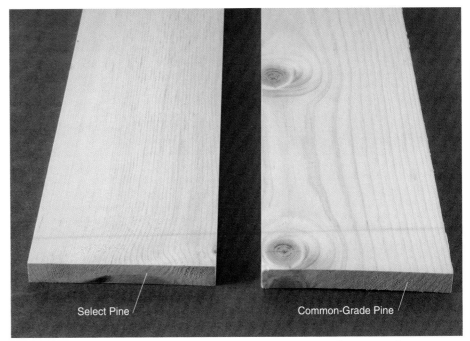

Clear, or select, pine, left, has few defects; common-grade pine, right, contains more knots and pitch pockets.

Select Pine

Common-Grade Pine

Molding Types. When it comes to choosing molding, the choices are slightly different. It is difficult, if not impossible, to find molding profiles cut from common-grade lumber. Clear-grade lumber is used for most profiles because knots and sap pockets would create inevitable holes in the molding and can dull expensive cutters. Clear-grade material is suitable for both stain-grade and painted finishes.

Finger-Jointed Molding. If you are looking to save some money, and your job is definitely going to be painted, you can consider finger-jointed molding. This term describes molding stock that has been built up of short lengths of lumber. The ends of each short piece are machined in an interlocking finger profile and glued together. The built-up lumber is then run through a molder, just like clear stock, and the profile is cut.

The use of short pieces of lumber saves money. In this process, no effort is made to match the color or grain of the lumber, but knots and other defects are excluded. As a result, you can use this stock for paint-grade work and save quite a bit on the cost of material; however, finger-jointed stock is usually only offered in the most common molding profiles. Many suppliers now apply a primer coat to their finger-jointed stock, so you can save both money and labor by using this material.

Finger Joint

Stock Molding Primer

Most lumberyards and home centers provide a display with a sample of available molding profiles. Each retailer has a selection of moldings that they carry as stock items, and while most are similar, you may find more profiles at one dealer over another. Moldings that are manufactured by one of the large millwork suppliers will be identical from one source to another, but those that are turned out by a local millwork house might not exactly match those of another manufacturer. In other words, a colonial casing from your local home center may not match the one from Johnny's Lumber Barn, despite having the same descriptive name. Because of this possible discrepancy, it is best to purchase all of each molding profile from one supplier.

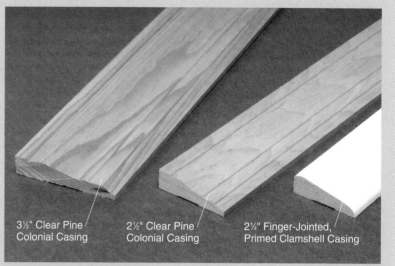

3½" Clear Pine Colonial Casing

2½" Clear Pine Colonial Casing

2¼" Finger-Jointed, Primed Clamshell Casing

Typical molding profiles available from most home centers include the casings shown above.

Poplar

Although pine is the primary softwood that is used for interior trim, poplar is a hardwood species that shares many of the qualities of pine, and it can be used in similar situations. Poplar is soft enough so that you can nail it without drilling pilot holes, and its closed-grain structure finishes well. The natural appearance of poplar can range from a warm cream color to a quite distinct green or purple, and it has a rather bland grain pattern, so it is most often painted. But if the material is carefully selected, you could use it with a stained finish. Poplar is frequently used by millwork houses for their custom paint-grade molding. It is a fast-growing species, and it is one of the least expensive hardwoods.

Red Oak

When home builders decide to provide an upgraded trim package, red oak is often their first choice of materials. Its open-grain structure can create bold contrast, especially when the wood is stained. But red oak also has a pleasant reddish-brown natural color, leaving open the option of treating it with a clear finish and no stain. Depending on the way the lumber is cut from the log, it can display a grain that is linear, with long parallel grain lines, or graphic, with peaked cathedral shapes that run the length of a board.

Because it is used extensively for interior trim, many of the stock profiles that are available in pine are also available in red oak.

TRIM TIP

If You Don't See It, Ask. If you do not see a molding profile on display that fits your needs, it is still possible that your retailer can obtain what you want. Most dealers have access to a more extensive selection of profiles than they choose to stock, so it's worth asking if they have a catalog of available moldings. Of course, expect to pay a premium for special orders, but in most cases, it will be less expensive than commissioning a custom molding.

Material and finish go hand-in-hand when designing a trim package. In the room shown opposite, white-painted wainscoting complements the wall color.

Painted finishes, top right, are usually applied to molding made from softwood.

The Back Side of Molding

When you examine most commercial molding, especially those pieces wider than 2 inches, you will notice that the back side has been slightly hollowed out. This relief cut serves two purposes. First, by reducing the thickness, it helps to lessen the tendency of the stock to cup. And, second, it allows the molding to bridge any irregularities in the wall surface and stay tight at the outside edges—where it counts.

Relief Cuts

Wide moldings often have relief cuts on the back. The hollowed-out sections help reduce cupping.

Hardwood versus Softwood

In a home center, poplar and other hardwood boards are often sold according to the same system that is used for softwood lumber. In this convention, boards are given a nominal size description—1x2, 1x4, etc.—that corresponds to the size of the board that is rough-sawn at the mill before it is planed smooth. The actual size of the board that you purchase is always less than the nominal size. For instance, the 1x2 and 1x4 boards are actually ¾ x 1½ inches and ¾ x 3½ inches. These boards are sold in even foot lengths from 6 to 16 feet.

If you shop for material at a hardwood lumberyard, however, you will find another classification system. Hardwood lumber is also classified according to the thickness of the material before it is planed smooth, but the descriptive categories are different. Trees are sawn at the mill into boards of varying thickness measured in quarters of an inch. For example, a board that is 1 inch thick would be called 4/4 stock and one 2 inches thick would be 8/4 stock. These rough-sawn boards are then dried and sold to a wholesaler or end user who planes them to a finished thickness. In addition, hardwood lumber is normally sold in boards of random width and length. So specifying the amount of material needed for a particular job requires a bit more effort and results in a greater amount of waste.

Rough-Cut Red Oak

S4S 1x6 Pine

Hardwood and softwood have different classification systems that denote stock size.

Hardwood Thickness Chart

Size Name	Rough Thickness	Planed Thickness
4/4	1"	$^{13}/_{16}$"
5/4	1¼"	$1^{1}/_{16}$"
6/4	1½"	$1^{5}/_{16}$"
8/4	2"	1¾"
10/4	2½"	$2^{5}/_{16}$"
12/4	3"	2¾"

Stains and clear finishes, right, are usually reserved for hardwoods.

Selecting Wood Moldings

Keep in mind that although each molding profile usually has a particular use associated with it, you are not bound to use it in any specific way. For example, it is not unusual to find a baseboard profile used as a frieze board in a cornice. Or a panel molding can be added to a casing or chair rail to help create a distinctive look.

In addition, you can cut a stock molding apart and use just part of the profile, either alone or in combination with other pieces. This technique may require additional modification, such as planing the back flat, but it provides another tool for expanding your design options.

Built-Up Designs. Another option is to create designs using two, three, or even four common profiles in one assembly. Some examples are shown on page 16, but you can easily create your own designs with a little experimentation. By varying the use of moldings and combining them in layered assemblies, you can achieve a wide variety of effects that create extravagant architectural details or may go well beyond the obvious applications.

Custom Profiles. If you find that you cannot achieve the look you desire with stock molding, even by combining profiles, you can turn to a custom molding supplier. Most areas of the

Common Molding Profiles

1¾" Bed Molding

3⅝" Crown Molding

1¾" Picture Rail Molding

1⅝" Panel Molding

1⅜" Base Cap Molding

1⅛" Band Molding

⅞" Wall Molding

1¹⁄₁₆" Cove Molding

1⅛" Bullnose Stop Molding

1¹⁄₁₆" Shoe Molding

⅝" Quarter-Round Molding

2½" Chair Rail Molding

2¼" Colonial Casing

3¼" 3-Step Colonial Casing

3¼" Colonial Base

country have custom millwork shops that offer a wide selection of profiles, as well as the capability to match an existing molding or a drawing that you provide. And if you can't find a local supplier, there are plenty of shops that will ship anywhere in the country. Most have Web sites, so you can see molding samples and profile drawings to help you select your profiles.

As you might expect, having custom moldings made can be expensive—especially if a new cutter must be ground for the job. The cost for these services is based on a combination of material and labor costs to install the knives and run the molder—knife grinding is additional and is based on the size of the knife and depth of profile. Most of these shops have an extensive collection of molding cutters from past jobs that they can use. You would be well advised to examine their list of available profiles, to see if one can fit your job, before spending the additional dollars to have a new knife ground.

Once you enter the realm of custom molding, you open the door to a large world of material choices. Of course, for paint-grade work, poplar would be the first choice. But if you are attracted to a natural finish, you can consider any of the native or imported hardwoods that are becoming more popular due to their own distinct character, color, and grain.

Built-Up Molding Profiles

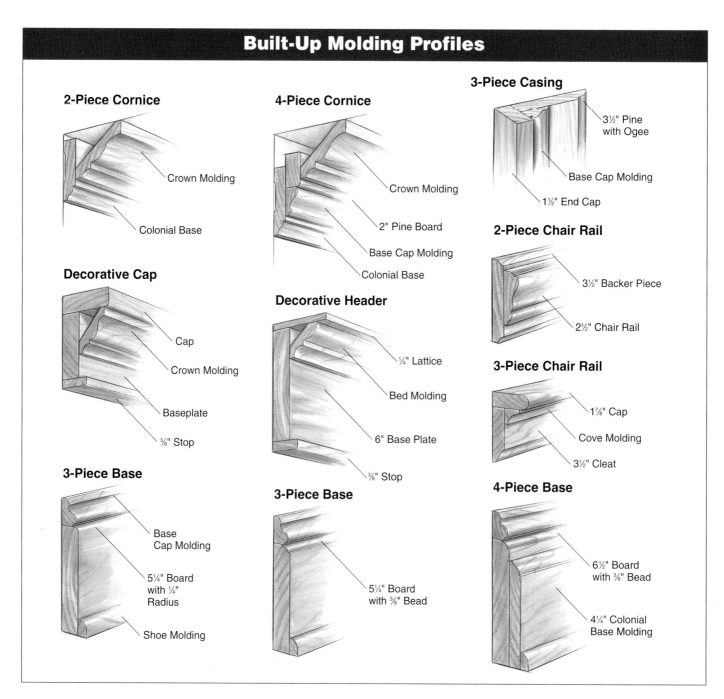

2-Piece Cornice
- Crown Molding
- Colonial Base

Decorative Cap
- Cap
- Crown Molding
- Baseplate
- ⅜" Stop

3-Piece Base
- Base Cap Molding
- 5¼" Board with ¼" Radius
- Shoe Molding

4-Piece Cornice
- Crown Molding
- 2" Pine Board
- Base Cap Molding
- Colonial Base

Decorative Header
- ¼" Lattice
- Bed Molding
- 6" Base Plate
- ⅜" Stop

3-Piece Base
- 5¼" Board with ⅜" Bead

3-Piece Casing
- 3½" Pine with Ogee
- Base Cap Molding
- 1½" End Cap

2-Piece Chair Rail
- 3½" Backer Piece
- 2½" Chair Rail

3-Piece Chair Rail
- 1⅞" Cap
- Cove Molding
- 3½" Cleat

4-Piece Base
- 6½" Board with ⅜" Bead
- 4¼" Colonial Base Molding

Hardwood Lumber Options

If you select a custom hardwood molding, you may need some matching lumber as well. In most cases, your local home center won't be much help in this regard. Sometimes a custom millwork house will supply lumber in a matching species, but some are not equipped to provide sales of plain lumber. The alternative source is a dedicated hardwood supplier. These dealers are often a bit more difficult to locate, because most of their customers are cabinet and furniture shops, but many are willing to sell to retail clients. And if you only need a small amount of lumber, you can always approach local woodworkers—more often than not they are happy to help out an enthusiastic do-it-yourselfer. When all else fails, there are many lumber dealers who will ship material anywhere in the country. Just remember to factor in the cost of shipping when you put together your budget.

In broad terms, hardwoods are divided into those with an open grain and those with a closed-grain structure. Woods with open grain include ash, red and white oak, walnut, butternut, elm, and mahogany. Some of these species feature a distinct difference in the density of the early and late seasonal growth that makes up each annual ring. As a result, when the wood is sliced, it displays a characteristic coarse appearance with alternating dense and porous grain. When these woods are stained, the open grain readily absorbs the color, while the dense areas are more resistant. This can create a striking effect, but for some situations it may appear too busy. Other open-grained woods have a more uniform grain, but one

that is nonetheless porous, causing uneven absorption of the finish. When preparing an open-grained wood for a smooth finish, you should apply paste grain filler to fill the more porous areas of the wood surface. This technique prevents the finish material from being absorbed into the grain, which would otherwise leave a textured coating on the surface.

Closed-grain woods include birch, cherry, hard and soft maple, poplar, gum, and sycamore. These are woods of more uniform density and, except for figured varieties, generally present a quieter and more reserved appearance than the open-grained woods.

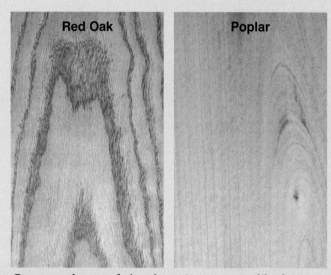

Open-grain wood absorbs stains more readily than closed grain. Red oak is open grain; poplar is closed grain.

Painted finishes, right, work well on both softwood and hardwood.

Characteristics of Lumber

Whether you are dealing with molding or flat lumber, wood is a dynamic material. Although it is solid and hard, it is not a static substance, and it responds to fluctuations in temperature and humidity by expanding, contracting, cupping, and warping. The degree to which any piece of wood reacts to changing conditions is dependent on a number of factors, and the study of this subject has filled many volumes. But for the purpose of trim installation, some basic knowledge can be useful.

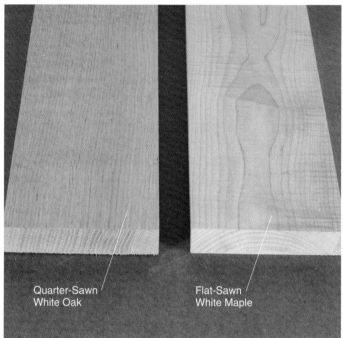

Quarter-Sawn
White Oak

Flat-Sawn
White Maple

Note the grain pattern of the samples of quarter-sawn and flat-sawn lumber shown above.

Quarter-Sawn Lumber. When boards are cut from a log, the orientation of the grain in the boards is determined by the way that the growth rings intersect the board surface. At one extreme is a quarter-sawn board in which the rings are perpendicular to the surface; this is also called vertical grain. To manufacture quarter-sawn lumber, the boards are sawn perpendicular to the exterior of the log. In this process, the yield from the log is reduced and the boards are relatively narrow. The stock displays straight, parallel grain lines on a board surface and, in some species like oak, characteristic rays become visible. These boards resist cupping and warping, and they are less likely to swell and contract than flat-sawn stock. Because there is more waste and also higher labor costs involved in cutting quarter-sawn lumber, it commands a premium price.

Flat-Sawn Lumber. In flat-sawn lumber, the boards are cut parallel with one side of a log, and the growth rings intersect the surface at a more acute angle. This technique provides the best yield from a log, but the lumber is less stable than quarter-sawn, and the grain patterns are more variable. In practice, much lumber falls somewhere between true vertical grain and flat-sawn patterns. If you have the luxury of examining a pile of lumber to make your selection, you can often select boards with similar grain for a particular project.

Complementary trim is used to highlight the newel posts at left.

TRIM TIP

Back Priming. Wood expands and contracts as moisture is absorbed or lost from its cell structure. And when you use any wood in a project, anything you can do to minimize that movement will create a better result—less splitting of the stock and tighter joints. One simple technique you can use is to make sure that all surfaces of your trim are sealed. For paint-grade work, simply apply a coat of paint or primer to the back side of the stock before installing it. For parts that will receive a stained or clear finish, apply a coat of varnish or polyurethane—stain alone is not a good sealer. This technique is especially important in areas that are subject to high humidity, such as kitchens, bathrooms, and utility rooms.

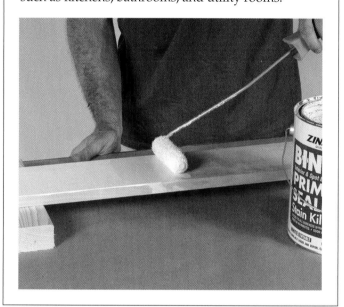

Back primed trim is destined for high-humidity areas.

Expansion and Contraction. Movement due to expansion or contraction occurs almost exclusively across the grain of a board, and not along its length. For practical purposes, the majority of trim applications will not be greatly affected by this movement, as most details are constructed of narrow pieces where the movement is negligible. However, you will notice that wooden doors and windows tend to swell in the hot and humid summer months and then contract in the winter. Another case where wood movement must be taken into account is when you install a shoe molding around a hardwood floor. In this situation, it is important that you nail the molding to the baseboard instead of the floor boards so that the boards can expand and contract independent of the molding. And if wide, solid wood panels are used in a wainscot application, it is also important to design the installation so that the panels can expand and contract without cracking or showing gaps.

Molding details enliven simple square columns.

Other Trim Materials

Although most people think of wood when the subject of trim arises, these days there are other options. When a job is destined to be painted, you can consider molding made of composite wood materials or even plastics.

Medium-Density Fiberboard.

Medium-density fiberboard, or MDF, is a product that is made from ground wood fibers bound with adhesive under pressure. The resulting material is uniformly dense and very stable. Manufacturers can mill the raw material, much like wood, into various profiles, and the resulting moldings have an exceptionally smooth surface. Most of these moldings are primed at the factory, providing an excellent base for a painted finish. The extreme density of MDF makes it quite a bit heavier than a comparable piece of wooden molding; and it must be treated much like hardwood, in that you need to drill

pilot holes before nailing. Because it has no grain structure, the edges of cuts tend to be pretty delicate, and the material can chip easily when fitting an intricate joint; use extra care in those situations.

Resin Moldings. *Polyurethane* and *polystyrene* moldings provide another option for paint-grade jobs. These products are especially attractive for ceiling moldings because they are extremely lightweight and install very easily. Plastic moldings can be cast in a wide variety of shapes, and extremely large and elaborate profiles are easy to achieve. For the installer, you eliminate the need for cutting coped joints at inside corners, as the plastic resin cannot be worked like wood. Instead, these intersections are treated with miter joints and any gaps must be filled with joint compound or caulk.

Some resin moldings are designed for use in curved applications. They are flexible enough so

that you can bend them to fit a concave or convex wall surface. There are also manufacturers that will cast these moldings to fit an arched or elliptical opening. For these situations, you would need to specify the dimensions of the opening, or send a template, to have the pieces made. Most of these systems use a combination of adhesives and nails to hold them in place, and they generally come primed to accept either a painted or opaque stain finish.

If you are looking for columns or ornamental pedestals to bring classical style to a room, you might look at some in fiberglass instead of wood. In most cases, a polymer column is less expensive than one of wood, and it typically requires less maintenance—especially if you are considering a damp location such as the kitchen or bath. These products are offered in both stock and custom sizes so that almost any situation can be accommodated.

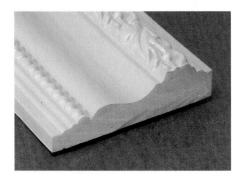

Resin molding, above, can be installed with nails and glue like traditional wood molding.

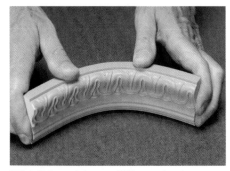

Flexible resin molding, above, can be bent to match most curved walls—either concave or convex surfaces.

Resin moldings come in hundreds of profiles and designs. The room above contains resin crown, casing, and panels.

Making Your Own Molding

Commercial molding manufacturers use heavy duty molders and shapers to produce the different profiles they offer. Working at home, you cannot expect to duplicate that capability. However, with a router and small table saw, you can produce a modest selection of moldings to function as elements of window and door trim, chair rail, baseboard, or wainscoting.

For a few small pieces of molding, use a hand-held router to cut the profile. Clamp a board to the worktable to keep the stock secure while routing. You may need to place spacer blocks beneath the board to provide clearance for the ball bearing pilot. Allow the router to get up to full speed before starting the cut. Then advance the tool along the edge to cut the molded shape.

Router Tables. If you need a lot of molding, the easier method is to mount the router in a router table. Commercial router tables are available in a variety of prices and configurations, some for tabletop use and others that are freestanding. Whatever type of table you use, make sure that it is either clamped firmly to a worktable or screwed to the floor to keep it from moving around while you work.

If you examine a catalog of router bits, you might be surprised at the number of different profiling bits that are available. Some of the larger bits are only available with a ½-inch-diameter shank, and require a heavy-duty router for safe use, but many are suitable for smaller routers that accept bits with a ¼-inch-diameter shank.

Mount your chosen bit in the router, and install the router in the table. Adjust the height of the tool, and then set the fence to expose the desired profile. Even though many bits have a ball-bearing pilot guide, it is safest to use a fence on the router table—the face of the fence should align exactly with the bearing. Adjust the guard on the table to cover the spinning bit and install finger-board hold-downs to keep the stock pushed tight to the table surface.

For the safest procedure, do not attempt to cut a molding profile on a narrow board. Instead, cut the molding on the edge of a wide board. Then use the table saw to rip the profile off the edge. Repeat the procedure for each piece you need. When the board gets too narrow, put it aside for another use.

1 To make a narrow molding, first rout the desired profile on the edge of a wide board. Use a bit with a ball-bearing guide, or install an accessory edge guide to determine the position of the bit. Make a test cut on some scrap stock to be sure that adjustments are correct; then cut the profile on the edge of the stock.

2 Use the table saw to rip the narrow molding from the edge of the wide board. If possible, use a finger-board hold-down jig to exert even pressure on the board and prevent kickbacks. The hold-down jig also eliminates any need to position your fingers near the blade. Always use a push stick as you reach the end of the cut.

Panel Materials

Panel stock is most often carried in thicknesses of ¼, ½, and ¾ inch, although it is manufactured in sheets as thin as ⅛ inch and as thick as 1½ inches. When you shop for this material, you will find that a variety of core options are available. Traditional plywood has a *veneer core*—formed from thin layers of wood pressed together—with a decorative veneer on each face. The grain of each layer is arranged at 90 degrees to that of the adjacent layer, so the panel is dimensionally stable. One drawback to traditional plywood is that these panels often do not stay flat, especially after they are cut. In a wainscot application where the material will be fastened to a wall, this is usually not a problem, but for other jobs this can be troublesome.

MDF Panels. Some panels are made with a *medium-density fiberboard* (MDF) *core*. A mixture of wood fibers and glue that is pressed together and heated, MDF is extremely smooth and uniformly dense. An MDF panel without a face veneer is considerably cheaper than a sheet of plywood and provides an excellent surface for a painted finish. The price of an MDF panel with a face veneer is usually close to that of a plywood panel, but it is more likely to remain flat when cut into workable parts. If you are buying MDF panels for a job, you should plan to have a helper to handle the material, as it is extremely heavy. Also, the nature of the core is such that machining it yields a lot of very fine dust. So be prepared with dust masks, eye protection, and a good shop vacuum.

Particleboard Cores. Panels with a *particleboard core* are another option. The construction of these panels is similar to that of MDF-core stock, except that the core consists of flakes of softwood lumber and glue. These panels are also formed under heat and pressure, and while quite stable, they do not feature a particularly uniform core. As with MDF panels, these are sold with and without a face veneer, but the raw panels are not as well suited to paint-grade use. In general, these are a less desirable choice for a wainscoting application.

Lumber-Core Panels. *Lumber-core* panels are the elite class of manufactured panel stock. Strips of solid lumber are glued together and covered with a thick layer of veneer called cross-banding. The face veneer is then applied to each side of this sandwich to yield the finished product. Because this is a premium product, and is most often used in furniture manufacture, you would need to obtain this type of panel by special order—and expect to pay a premium price. It is not unusual for a lumber-core panel to cost twice the price of a comparable plywood panel.

Advances in technology have yielded a number of composite *multi-core* panels, which mix different materials in the core in an effort to reduce weight and cost while maintaining a stable product. One of these products uses the idea of traditional plywood, but alternates layers of wood and MDF. Another panel features a core of particleboard covered by thick cross-bands under the face veneer.

Manufactured Panel Core Materials

- Multi-Core
- MDF Core
- Particleboard Core
- Lumber Core
- Veneer Core

Panel Faces

The veneers that are applied to panel faces can display various patterns, depending on the way that they were cut from the log and joined together. Some veneers are peeled from a log that is mounted on a huge lathe. These are called *rotary-cut* veneers, and they show a characteristic grain pattern that is rather wild. In some species, a rotary-cut veneer can feature grain that moves in a zigzag pattern down the sheet. Rotary veneers can be very large, and often one sheet can cover an entire panel.

Some veneers are sliced or sawn into sheets that are parallel with one side of a tree; these are called plain-sliced veneers, and they usually show cathedral shaped grain patterns. Plain-sliced veneers are often *book-matched,* or joined together so that symmetrical patterns appear across the panel. *Quartersawn* veneer is cut parallel with the radius of the log. These veneers show straight grain, and in some oak species, characteristic ray flake.

When shopping for panel stock, pay close attention to the veneer on the face. If you need more than one panel, try to select them so that the veneers are close in color and grain pattern. Whatever type of panel you select, inspect the face for any defects such as torn out veneer, wood-filler patches, and deep scratches. For use in wainscoting, you only need material with one good face, so if available, purchase stock with a back veneer of inferior grade to save some money.

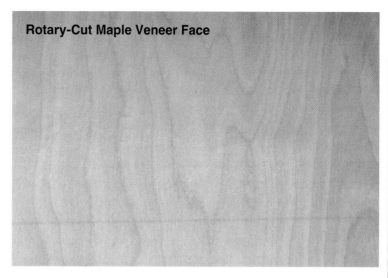

Rotary-Cut Maple Veneer Face

Book-Matched Cherry Veneer Face

Quartersawn White Oak Veneer Face

Materials and finish selection, left, contribute to the distinctive look of this staircase.

Fasteners

Fasteners are an essential part of trim work. Almost every process demands that you use some type of mechanical fastener to hold a molding to a surface or join two pieces of wood. The primary fastener for trim is the finishing nail. These nails feature a relatively narrow shaft with a slightly larger head. Typically, the head has a small dimple in the top surface to engage the tip of a nail set. Select an appropriately sized nail for each task—for example, for fastening trim boards to framing members, the nail should enter the framing member at least 1 inch. Remember to take the thickness of the drywall or plaster surface into account.

For fastening small pieces of molding, wire nails, or brads, are often used. These are essentially very fine finishing nails available in sizes between ⅝ and 1½ inches long.

The nails that are used in nail guns are classified in the same manner as traditional finishing nails, but they are slightly different in configuration. With normal nails, as the length of a fastener increases, the diameter also gets larger. But the nails for a nail gun are of one constant diameter, regardless of the length. Consequently, a nail gun can drive a long nail and still leave a relatively small-diameter hole.

Screws. Screws are another important fastener. For many years, brass screws with slotted heads were the norm for woodworking, but the expense and relative soft nature of brass have made these obsolete except for decorative applications. And the popularity of power screw drivers has almost eliminated the slot head, replacing it with the more reliable Phillips and Robertson (square drive) styles.

Screws are available with round, oval, flat, and bugle-head styles. If you need your screw to sit flush with the wood surface, or want it completely hidden by a plug or filler, you should choose flat or bugle-head styles. Next, select the screw material.

Finishing nails have a dimple on top to hold a nail set. When installing molding, the nail should penetrate into the underlying framing by at least 1 in.

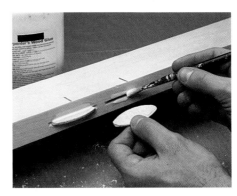

When covered with glue and inserted into the slot cut by a plate joiner, joining plates provide a reliable fastening option.

Nail Sizes

Nail Size	Length
3d	1¼"
4d	1½"
6d	2"
8d	2½"
10d	3"
12d	3¼"
16d	3½"

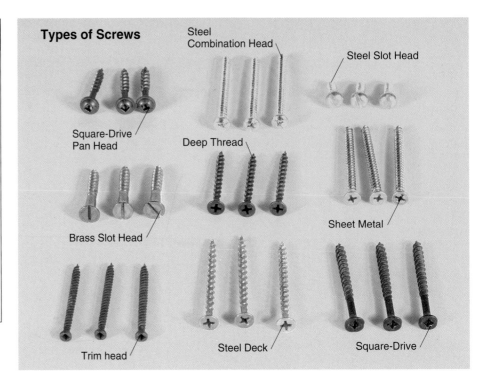

Types of Screws

Steel Combination Head

Steel Slot Head

Square-Drive Pan Head

Deep Thread

Brass Slot Head

Sheet Metal

Trim head

Steel Deck

Square-Drive

Plain steel screws are the least expensive alternative, but hardened steel offers a tougher screw that is less likely to snap under pressure or strip out if the driver slips. Finally, consider the style of the screw body. Traditional wood screws have a body with threads that only extend about two-thirds of the way up the shank, and the body tapers from the head to the tip. Sheet metal and deep-thread styles have bodies of constant diameter, and the threads extend farther

up the screw. Trim-head screws have small-diameter heads that can be used like finishing nails.

Dowels. Dowels are wooden cylinders of a specific diameter that are coated with glue and inserted in matching holes in the two sides of a joint. For commercial applications, dowels are available in precut lengths with either spiral or longitudinal grooves down the dowel length. These grooves provide a means for

excess glue to escape the hole. If you are using plain dowel stock, it is a good practice to carve one or two shallow grooves down the length of each dowel with a knife or chisel.

Joining Plates. These are football-shaped wafers of compressed wood. They are designed to fit into matching semicircular slots that are cut in each side of a joint using a plate joiner. Joining plates come in three standard sizes.

Using Hollow-Wall Anchors

It's always preferable to fasten trim parts to the framing inside a wall or ceiling, but there are times when there is no stud, plate, or joist where you need one. In those situations you have two options. You can rip into the wall and install some blocking, or you can use one of the various hollow-wall anchors to install your part.

1 Drill through the piece to be installed using a countersink bit. The bit will mark the drywall for drilling.

2 Remove the molding, and drill pilot holes. Insert anchors into the pilot holes.

3 Attach molding, and cover screw heads with dowels. Trim the dowels, and finish the workpiece.

Glue and Construction Adhesives

In the pursuit of tight, strong joints, woodworking adhesives are an important addition to your arsenal of tools. The standard glues for most joints are *polyvinyl acetate (PVA) adhesives,* known casually as *white* and *yellow* glues. While the white variety can be used for most porous materials, the yellow variety—also called aliphatic resin glue—has been specifically formulated for woodworking applications. Brown-colored versions are available for use with woods of darker tone. For applications that need water resistance, there are formulations of yellow glue that are rated as *waterproof.* These glues are technically known as cross-linking PVA. They are easy to use, nontoxic, and clean up easily with water before curing.

Polyurethane adhesives also offer water resistance and are compatible with a number of different materials. One unique feature of this glue is that it requires moisture to cure, so it is often recommended that you slightly dampen the wood surface before applying the glue. This glue tends to foam up as it cures, and it can be difficult to clean up a joint without leaving a residue. In addition, polyurethane glue will stain your skin, so you need to wear gloves when working with it.

Epoxies are available in a variety of formulas with different strengths and setting times. These adhesives require that you mix a hardener with a resin to start the chemical

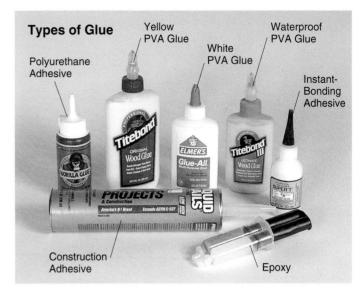

Types of Glue

reaction that cures the epoxy. Quick-setting versions are sold in convenient double-tube dispensers that provide the proper ratio of hardener to resin. For joints that require the highest bonding strength, especially in varied materials, epoxy is the best choice. But epoxy is also a toxic material, so be sure to wear gloves and a respirator to protect yourself from exposure.

Instant-bonding adhesives, sometimes called "super glue," have limited use in woodworking, but there are times when they can be a life-saver. Technically called

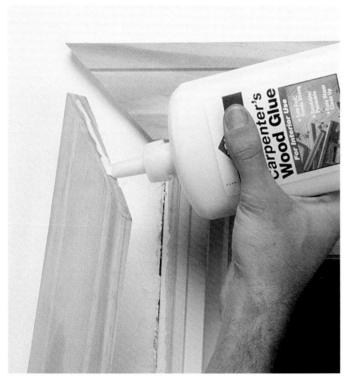

For tight joints, apply a bead of glue to miter cuts. Complete the job using finishing nails.

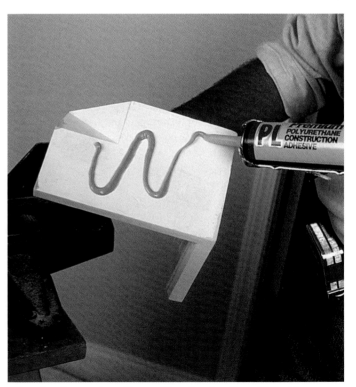

Standard construction adhesive is often all that is required for applying resin-type moldings.

Types of Sandpaper

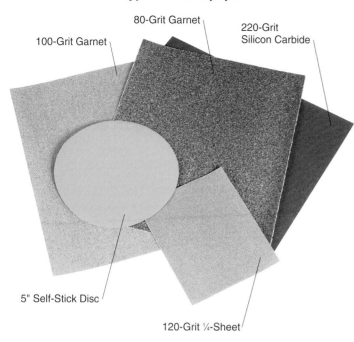

100-Grit Garnet

80-Grit Garnet

220-Grit Silicon Carbide

5" Self-Stick Disc

120-Grit ¼-Sheet

cyanoacrylate adhesive, this glue sets in a matter of seconds, so clamping is virtually unnecessary. This adhesive can be very useful to repair small chips and torn-out grain in a wood surface.

Construction adhesive is a thick-bodied substance that comes in a tube for use in a caulk gun. There are different formulations of adhesive for specific uses such as bonding paneling or drywall, or resin molding installation.

Sandpaper

It's rare to find someone who truly enjoys sanding, but it is an important part of most woodworking projects, and if approached methodically, it need not be a particularly tedious or difficult task. The first step is to have the right material for the job, and that means sandpaper.

You will see sandpaper that is manufactured with different abrasives, and each has its preferred use. Garnet paper is best for sanding by hand. Machine sanding requires a longer lasting, tougher abrasive, and aluminum oxide is generally considered the best choice. Silicone carbide paper is a good choice for sanding finishes between coats as it holds up well in fine grits.

Sandpaper is rated according to the coarseness of the abrasive particles and type of backer. Lower grit numbers correspond to coarser abrasive. You can find papers rated from 40 to 1500 grit, but for general trim projects, your most frequent selections will fall between 100 and 220 grit. Backers for sandpaper can be either cloth or paper, with paper more common in sheets and discs, and cloth most prevalent in belts. The weight of the backer is classified from "A" to "X" with "A" being the thinnest and most flexible. For hand sanding, "A" weight

is most appropriate, and for orbital machine sanding "C" weight is best.

Sandpaper is sold in full sheets of 9 x 11 inches, as well as in ¼- and ½-sheet sizes for pad sanders. You will also find discs and belts of various sizes to fit different types of power sanders. Most discs come with a backing of Velcro or pressure-sensitive adhesive for mounting to the sanding pad.

Caulk

For jobs that are destined to be painted, caulk can be the trim carpenter's best friend. But it's also important to realize that caulk is not a replacement for doing a careful job of fitting and assembling joints. Although we generally think of walls and ceilings as flat, in most cases you will find dips and humps in these surfaces. And when trim is applied, there is sometimes a small gap between the two materials. These are the places where caulk is an indispensable tool. A judicious application of caulk can blend an applied molding to a wall or ceiling surface, creating a seamless appearance. Small gaps in trim joints, especially at inside corners of baseboards and cornices, can also be filled with caulk.

Acrylic latex caulk is the best all-around choice for interior trim work. This material is easy to apply, and you can shape a caulk joint with a wet finger or putty knife. It cleans up with water while still fresh, and it readily accepts a painted finish after proper curing. Expect latex caulk to shrink a bit as it cures, so for wide joints you might have to reapply the material before painting. For best results, prime the woodwork and wall or ceiling surface before applying the caulk.

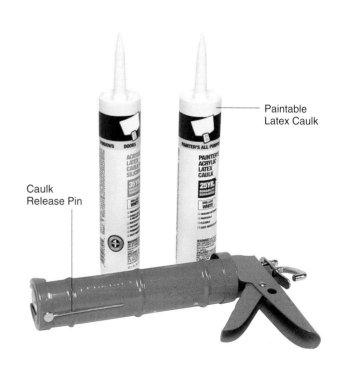

Paintable Latex Caulk

Caulk Release Pin

tools for trimwork

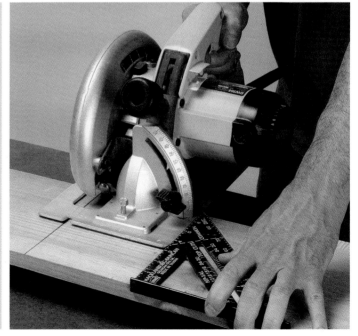

Measuring and Layout Tools

Your choice of measuring tools for any task depends, at least partially, on the scale of the job and tolerances you must keep. The secondary factor has to do with personal preference, for often there is a choice of appropriate tools. As you work with a variety of tools, you will naturally gravitate toward some over others. Just make sure that your preference for comfort or convenience does not result in a sacrifice of accuracy.

When it comes to marking stock to be cut to size, or laying out more complex joints, the accuracy of your marks is critical. Although the tool most associated with carpentry layout is the flat carpenter's pencil, this tool is really not very useful for trimwork. The thick, soft lead of the pencil and its fat body make it awkward to use and prone to rapid dulling; the result is a wide, vague mark. For trimwork the better choice is a hard pencil—#3 is perfect—that can be sharpened to a very fine point. If you keep a fine point on the tool, it will provide you with an extremely precise mark.

For the finest work, even a sharpened pencil mark can be too vague. In those situations where you want the highest degree of accuracy, a knife mark is the best choice. The type of knife you use is not important—an inexpensive utility knife will work as well as a fancy rosewood-handled layout knife—but the edge and tip should be razor sharp.

Measuring Tapes

A *measuring tape* is a great device for estimating materials and laying out a job. The most common sizes of steel retractable tape are ¾ inch wide by 12 or 16 feet long and 1 inch wide by 25 feet long, although reel-style tapes are available to 100-foot lengths. For room measurements and all-around general use, the 1-inch by 25-foot model is your best bet. The wide blade will support itself over a long span, and most rooms are less

Add an Inch. After some use, the hook on the end of the tape can become bent, worn, or have excess play, resulting in less-than-accurate readings. When close tolerances are involved, try a professional cabinet-maker's trick. Rather than measuring from the end of the tape, start your measurement at the 1 inch mark. Just remember to subtract that inch from the reading at the opposite end.

than 25 feet in length. Most have a locking lever that keeps the blade from retracting. Tapes usually have each "foot" mark clearly delineated as well as arrows or other indications for 16-inch spacing—this is especially handy for stud locations. You will typically find graduations down to ¹⁄₁₆ inch, with some models having ¹⁄₃₂-inch graduations for the first foot of the tape.

Folding Stick Rules

The *folding stick rule* is one of carpentry's oldest measuring devices and still very useful. These come in 6- and 8-foot lengths that fold into a compact 8-inch-long package. A stick rule is great for those situations where you need to measure something that is just out of reach, and you need to suspend the ruler over an unsupported space. It is also handy to gauge the extent of an overhanging detail or to measure the inside dimension of an opening. Most models have a sliding extension at one

end for easy inside measuring. For easy folding, periodically apply a tiny drop of oil to each folding joint.

Steel Rulers

Steel rulers usually come in sizes from 6 inches to 24 inches, although a yardstick could easily be included in this category. For the most accurate measurements, it's hard to beat a steel ruler because the graduations are scribed or etched into the surface, and they are, typically, finer lines than those painted on a wooden ruler or tape. In addition, it's easy to find rulers that have graduations as fine as ¹⁄₆₄ inch.

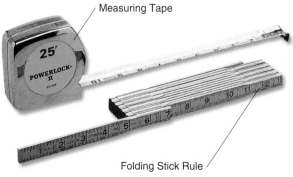

Measuring Tape

Folding Stick Rule

Squares

A *square* is the primary tool for testing that two edges are perpendicular, but it is also important for layout. Squares are available in different sizes and configurations for various uses.

Framing Square. This tool is made of steel or aluminum and has legs of 16 and 24 inches. In addition to inch measurements along each blade, you will find a chart for determining the angles for rafters of various slope roofs. A framing square is handy for laying out stud walls, but it is also useful in trim-work to check that larger panels are square or for testing door and window openings. Smaller squares are also available for close-in work.

Sliding Combination Square. In addition to being a precision square, this tool has a milled edge on the body that sits at 45 degrees to the blade for testing miter cuts. The body can slide along the graduated blade and lock in place at different settings so that you can use it as a depth or marking gauge. Most models also include a steel scriber and a small level vial on the body.

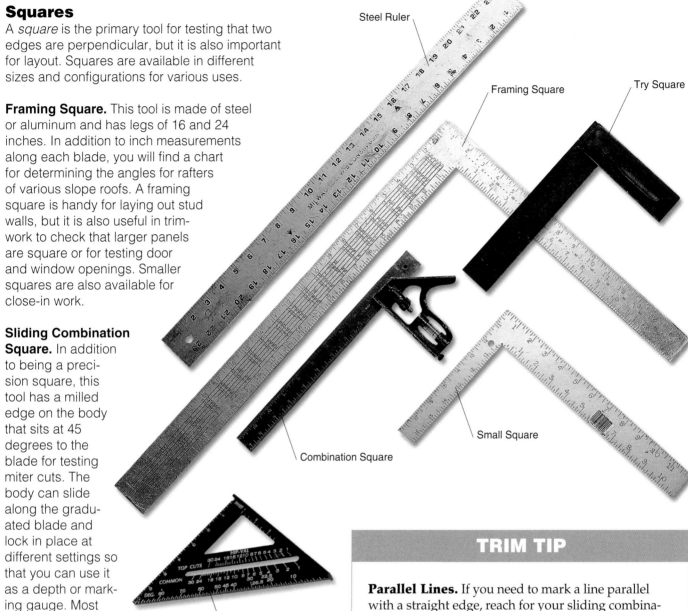

Steel Ruler

Framing Square

Try Square

Combination Square

Small Square

Speed Square

Try Square. This tool has a 6- or 8-inch blade with a fixed body. These are convenient for testing the accuracy of cuts on small parts. For the highest degree of accuracy, you can purchase an *engineer's precision square*. These steel squares are available in blade sizes from 6 to 12 inches and are guaranteed to conform to extremely fine tolerances (typically .016mm).

Speed Square. Although designed as a rafter layout tool, a speed square is valuable in trim work. You can use the speed square as a crosscutting guide for the circular saw to help in making square cuts on narrow lumber.

TRIM TIP

Parallel Lines. If you need to mark a line parallel with a straight edge, reach for your sliding combination square. Slide the body along the blade until you reach the distance your line needs to be from the edge. Hold the body along the edge and your sharpened pencil against the end of the blade. Slide both square and pencil down the edge to scribe your line.

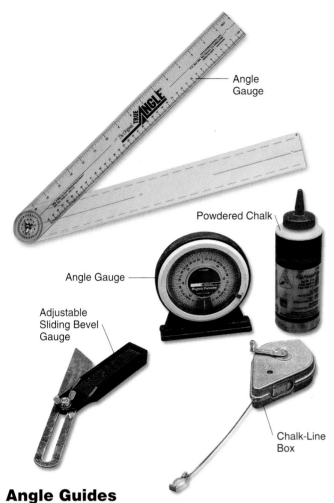

Angle Gauge

Angle Gauge

Powdered Chalk

Adjustable Sliding Bevel Gauge

Chalk-Line Box

Good Marks. When marking a board to be cut to length or determining a guideline on a wall, place a "V" at the desired mark rather than a vague line. Use the point of the "V" to indicate the exact point of measurement; then use a square, protractor, or straightedge to lay out the cut or layout line.

Angle Guides

Things would be much simpler in trim work if all angles were either 90 or 45 degrees, but life is just not like that. So, in order to be able to work with various angles, you will need a *protractor* or *angle gauge*. The particular configuration of your tool is not critical, but it's worth investing in a steel tool rather than a plastic model.

Adjustable Sliding Bevel Gauge. An *adjustable sliding bevel gauge* has no graduations to indicate particular angle measurement, but it is a great device for copying any angle. Simply loosen the nut; hold the body against one side of the angle; and slide the blade until it rests against the opposite side of the angle. Tighten the blade to retain the setting. You can then use the gauge to trace the angle onto another surface for direct cutting or bisecting with a protractor.

Chalk Line

A *chalk-line box* is a simple, but very valuable, tool for marking a long straight line between distant points on a wall, floor, or ceiling. It consists of a metal or plastic enclosure with a reel that holds a cotton string; the string has a metal hook on its free end. Pour powdered chalk into the box, and extend the string between the points you wish to connect. Hold the string taut, and gently lift and release it so that it snaps once against the surface to mark the straight line.

Levels

The concepts of plumb and level are primary to good trim carpentry work. In carpentry terms, something is level when it is perfectly parallel with the ground, with no slope. Something is plumb when it is perfectly vertical. Plumb and level lines are always perpendicular to one another.

Spirit Level. The most common tool used to test these qualities is the *spirit level*. A spirit level has two or three fluid-filled arched vials, each with a small air bubble inside. Hold the level against a horizontal or vertical surface to check if it is plumb or level; the bubble should be exactly between the gauge marks. (See page 32.)

Water Level. A *water level* can be used to set a level mark at two distant points. It consists of a hose, filled almost completely with water, with transparent ends. If you hold both ends up, the waterline at one end will always be level to the waterline at the opposite end.

Laser Level. A *laser level* projects a horizontal or vertical beam of light. Some models are self-leveling, but on others you need to adjust the unit first with a vial gauge. Rotary models can project the beam on all four walls of a room at the same time. Once you have your level or plumb line established, you can place marks appropriately to guide your measurement or installation.

Plumb Bob. One of the oldest methods of gauging if something is plumb, or of striking a plumb line, is to use a *plumb bob*. This tool is simply a string with a pointed weight attached to one of its ends. Most bobs are fashioned of brass, and some of the old models can be quite decorative. If you suspend the bob from any point, you can always be sure that the string will describe a perfectly plumb line.

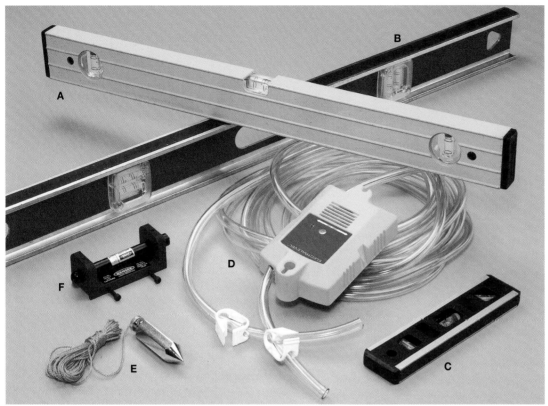

Levels:
A—2-ft. spirit level
B—4-ft. spirit level
C—6-in. spirit level
D—water level with electronic level sensor
E—plumb bob and string
F—laser level, which can be attached to a standard level

Stud Finder

Most trim carpentry involves attaching pieces of wood to a wall or ceiling surface. Because most rooms are finished with drywall or plaster, it is important to fasten parts to the underlying framing members whenever possible. While you can always poke holes to locate studs or joists, a much neater and quicker technique is to use a *stud finder*. Older models relied on magnets to sense nails or screws driven into the framing. Most electronic models have sensors that detect difference in capacitance to locate the studs. The most recent developments use a type of radar technology to sense the framing inside the wall. Electronic stud finders use a series of sounds or lights to indicate when the tool is directly over a stud.

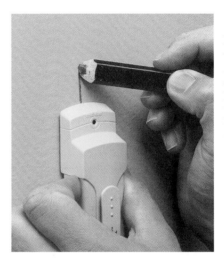

Stud finders help locate framing within a wall without damaging the surface of the wall. Most newer models use lights and sounds to indicate the location of the stud.

TRIM TIP

Making a Measuring Jig. Taking an accurate inside measurement—such as an exact window or door opening—is one of the challenges of trim work. To obtain exact measurements, take two sticks, each somewhat longer than one-half the overall dimension. Hold the sticks together and slide them apart until the ends touch the walls of the opening. Use clamps to lock the dimension; you can then use the guide to transfer the measurement to your trim piece.

Cutting Tools

For many specific jobs, as well as those times when an extension cord is not handy, a handsaw is the tool of choice. The saws most associated with the carpenter's trade are the traditional crosscut and rip saws. Each of these saws has a blade approximately 22 to 26 inches long that tapers from the handle toward the tip. A crosscut saw typically has 8 to 10 teeth per inch and a rip saw 4 to 5 teeth per inch. When using either of these saws, you should position yourself so that you can take long, straight strokes, with your arm and shoulder in line with the blade. If the saw is properly sharpened, you should not need to force the saw, but simply guide it back and forth, allowing the weight of the blade to determine the rate of cut.

A handy alternative to western-style hand saws is the Japanese Ryoba. This dual-purpose saw has fine crosscutting teeth on one edge and coarse ripping teeth on the opposite edge. All Japanese saws cut on the pull stroke, rather than the push stroke like western saws. This allows the saw blade to be thinner and therefore yields a smaller kerf, or width of cut. Using a Japanese style saw takes some practice, but once you master the technique, you will find it a very valuable addition to your toolbox.

Backsaw. A *backsaw* has a rectangular shaped blade with a steel or brass reinforcement along the top spine. The reinforcing spine allows the saw to have a thin blade that still stays straight. This type of saw comes in many sizes and tooth configurations, each with a particular use in mind. The smallest backsaws are called "dovetail" saws because they are designed to cut fine furniture joints called dovetails. Larger saws are handy for use in a miter box to cut molding to precise angles.

Coping Saw. A *coping saw* consists of a handle attached to a C-shaped frame. A thin blade is stretched between the ends of the frame. This configuration enables the user to make sharp turns with the saw to follow complex molding shapes. This tool is primarily used in the cutting of "coped" (or fitted) joints. Most carpenters install the blade so that the saw cuts on the "pull" stroke.

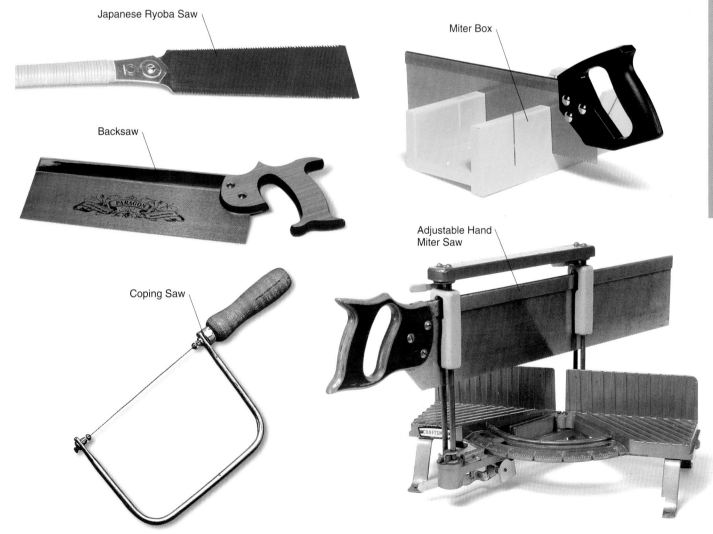

Japanese Ryoba Saw

Backsaw

Coping Saw

Miter Box

Adjustable Hand Miter Saw

Hand Chisels. A basic set of butt chisels, ranging in width from ¼ to 1½ inches, is a worthwhile investment for trimwork. You'll find them handy for fine paring of joints and cutting mortises for door hardware. In order to keep them sharp, purchase a good quality sharpening stone and honing guide—and use them often.

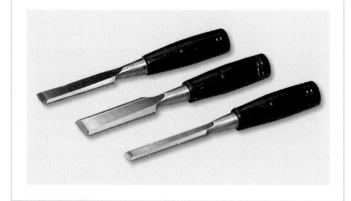

Circular Saw

Saber Saw

Miter Saws

If you only have a few miter joints to cut, it's hardly worth investing in a power miter saw. Fortunately, there are less expensive, and low-tech, alternatives—the wood or plastic miter box, and metal hand miter saw. The simplest tool for cutting simple miters is the *miter box*. A miter box has a U-shaped cross-section with saw kerfs cut at 45 and 90 degrees through the guide rails. These are meant to be used with a backsaw, which has a reinforcing spine along the top edge of the saw blade. You can find an inexpensive miter box, complete with back saw, at most home centers. Unfortunately, the miter box has the limitation of not allowing any adjustment in the angle of cut.

For more flexibility, you can turn to the *hand miter saw*. Some miter saws use a backsaw and some are designed to hold a saw that resembles a hacksaw. In either case, the saw is supported in a guide, and you have the ability to adjust the angle of cut from 45 degrees left to 45 degrees right, providing more flexibility than the miter box.

Power Cutting Tools

When you need a power saw for crosscutting or ripping solid lumber and sizing plywood panels, the *circular saw* is usually the first choice. Tool selection is based on the diameter of the cutting blade, and there are a number of sizes available. But for general use, pick a saw with a blade that is 7¼ inches in diameter, as this size should handle most cutting jobs. These models are adjustable for depth and angle of cut, and most will cut stock up to 2¼ inches thick at 90 degrees. Expect your saw to have a fixed upper blade guard and a lower retractable guard

that operates by spring tension. Some saws offer an electronic blade brake that stops the blade when you release the trigger, and this is a great option for increased safety. If it does not come with the saw, you should purchase an accessory rip guide for cutting strips of uniform width from wide stock. There are a number of different types of blades available for circular saws. Initially, you should purchase a combination blade for all-around use and a crosscutting blade for fine work.

Saber Saw. Sometimes called a *portable jig saw*, this is an extremely versatile tool that is great for cutting curved or intricate shapes. These tools accept a wide variety of blades for rough and finish cutting of wood, as well as plastics and metal. Most saws have an adjustable base for bevel cuts and a switch to allow the blade to move in either an orbital (for wood) or reciprocating (for plastic or metal) motion.

Power Miter Saws

When your trim projects become more extensive, a *power miter saw* will undoubtedly become one of the primary tools on the job. This is essentially a circular saw mounted on a pivoting stand. The motor and blade can swivel from side to side over the table to cut the desired angle. Most saws have preset detents at 90, 45, and 22.5 degrees.

Compound Miter Saws. These tools have the added capability for the blade to tip to one side to cut a bevel angle, in addition to the miter. A *sliding compound miter saw* adds one more feature to the mix by providing guide rails that allow the blade to be pulled through the cut, toward the operator. With sliding capability, these saws allow you to cut wide stock, cut joints on crown molding with the material held flat on the saw table, and cut grooves or tenon joints by limiting the depth of cut with a stop. Saws are available in a variety of sizes which are determined by blade diameter—most fall in the range of 8½- to 12-inch sizes. When selecting a saw, pay particular attention to the capacity ratings of each particular model—both the thickness and width of stock it will cut. While sliding compound saws are the most versatile of all miter saws, they are quite expensive; some models can exceed $600.

Power saws increase your versatility. Shown left and below are a standard miter saw and a sliding compound miter saw.

Shaping and Finishing Tools

Planes are one of the tools most often associated with carpentry. The image of the carpenter, with shavings flying, is almost an icon in woodworking. Aside from the image, however, the plane is a necessary part of your tool collection. While there are planes designed for many specific tasks, for a beginner approaching trimwork, a *block plane* will serve most purposes quite well. Block planes are about 6 inches long with a cutting iron approximately 1½ inches wide. The cutting iron is mounted, with the bevel facing up, at a low angle—this makes the tool especially well suited to trimming the end grain of a board, but it will also do a fine job planing the edge or face of a board.

You will find a block plane very handy for final fitting of a trim board to an uneven surface, or fine-tuning a miter joint. For best results, always keep the cutting iron razor sharp.

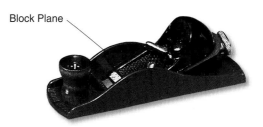

Block Plane

Sanders

For most people who work with wood, sanding is the least appealing part of any project—it is dusty and can be tedious—and it can seem hard to justify the effort. However, much of the final impression of a job lies in the quality of the finished surface, and sanding prepares the way for a first-class finish.

Belt Sanders. For the coarsest jobs, you can't beat a *belt sander* for fast stock removal. These tools usually accept 3- or 4-inch-wide belts in a variety of grits from very coarse (40 grit) to very fine (220 grit). A belt sander can be your best friend on a job, but it can also get out of control easily and do some damage. Make sure that you orient the sander so that the belt moves parallel with the grain, and always keep the machine moving down the length of the workpiece when the belt is running or you may gouge the surface.

Belt Sander

Random-Orbital Sanders

Orbital Sheet Sanders

Plate Joiner

You could easily spend years mastering the art of cutting various joints in wood—and many people have done just that. To do trimwork, you really do not have to master those skills. However, there are situations when you will need to join materials without screws or nails, and a simple, flexible approach can be found in plate joinery. Joining plates are football-shaped wafers of compressed wood, about ⅛ inch thick, that come in a variety of sizes. (See "Joining Plate Sizes," below.) To use the plates, cut a semicircular slot in each half of the joint with a *plate joiner*. The tool has a spinning blade that you advance into the wood to a preset depth. Location and alignment of the slot is controlled by two fences on the joiner, and there are adjustments that allow angle settings as well.

Once your joint is cut, spread a bit of glue into each slot and also on the surface of a joining plate. Push the plate into one of the matching slots, and assemble the joint. Use a clamp to hold the parts together while the glue sets. The glue causes the compressed wood of the plate to expand.

Joining plates have been dubbed "flat dowels" by some woodworkers, because they have largely replaced dowels as a means of joinery. Cutting a plate joint is much quicker than drilling matching dowel holes and has the added advantage of having some "play" in the joint. The slots are slightly longer than the plates, providing room to adjust a joint.

Random Orbital Sander. A *random orbital sander* is a finishing sander that has a disc-shaped pad. The sanding pad turns on an eccentric spindle so that it creates tiny swirl marks on the wood surface. This type of tool has the ability to remove stock quickly, but it also can leave a fine finish on the surface. Look for a model with a 5-inch-diameter pad because that size sanding disc is the most widely available.

Orbital Sheet Sanders. These tools have been the standard finishing sanders for many years. They are offered in ¼- and ½-sheet sizes and are generally the least expensive machine option for finish work. These sanders provide the best choice if you need to sand vertical surfaces.

Hand Sanding. Power sanders are great tools, but there are times when you just have to do the job by hand. For small, flat surfaces, you can use a block of wood as a sanding block. Or you can go the commercial route and purchase a rubber or cork block. For sanding molded profiles, use a bit of creativity to fashion a sanding block or pad that matches the profile. You could use a pencil or dowel as a backer to sand flutes in a pilaster, or a small can, jar, or the cardboard core from a roll of paper towels as a backer to sand a cove molding.

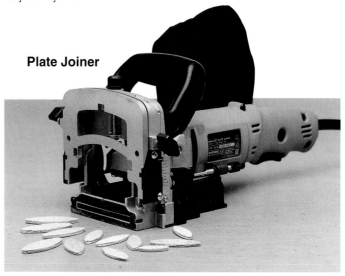

Plate Joiner

Joining Plate Sizes

#0: About ⅝ inch wide by 1¾ inches long (47 x 15 mm)

#10: About ¾ inch wide by 2⅛ inches long (53 x 19 mm)

#20: 1 inch wide by 2½ inches long (56 x 23 mm)

Using a Router Table

A router table has mounts to hold a router upside down. It's great for shaping wood that is too small to hold by hand. When facing the router, move the material from right to left.

Routers

A portable *router* gives you the ability to cut a wide range of molding profiles, as well as cutting grooves and trimming edges. Cutting bits are available in a dazzling array of profiles. Routers are rated by motor size and also by the size of the shank the collet (tool holder) will accept. For a first purchase, look for a model with a rating of 1½ to 1¾ horsepower with a ¼-inch collet. This is adequate for just about any task that you encounter and is a reasonable investment.

A basic router has a *fixed base* that requires you to set the depth of cut by turning a locking adjusting ring on the base; the depth must be set before turning on the tool. You will also see models that feature a *plunge base* that allows you to lower a spinning bit into the work surface. While a plunge-base router is the more flexible tool, it is a bit less stable than a comparable fixed-base tool. For molding edges, either type of base is fine, but for stopped internal flutes or grooves, you will need a plunge-base machine.

When using a router, always move the tool against the direction of rotation of the bit. As a general rule, this means that if you are facing the edge to be cut, the router should be guided from your left to your right.

If your router does not come with an accessory edge guide, you should certainly consider purchasing one. Many bits feature a ball-bearing pilot to guide the cut, but if you want to use other bits, the guide is almost a necessity.

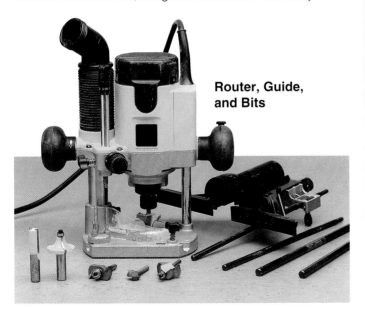

Router, Guide, and Bits

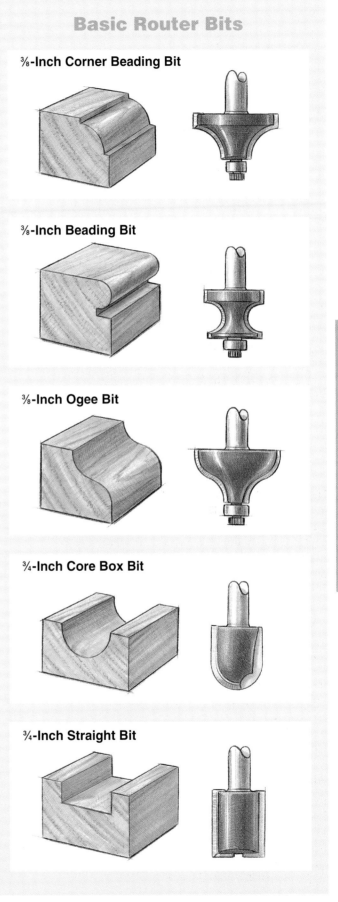

⅜-Inch Corner Beading Bit

⅜-Inch Beading Bit

⅜-Inch Ogee Bit

¾-Inch Core Box Bit

¾-Inch Straight Bit

Files and Rasps

Trimwork sometimes involves delicate fitting of two wood parts together, or one piece of wood against another surface such as plaster, drywall, brick, or stone. In those cases, the only true rule is to use the tool that works best—sometimes it could be a saw, others a knife, and still other times a file or rasp could be just right. *Files* and *rasps* come in a wide variety of shapes that make them perfect for the final fitting of coped joints, especially those that involve a complex profile.

One of the frequent challenges that can arise when casing a door or window is that the drywall will bulge out into the room, creating a hump in the wall surface. This situation is a natural by-product of taping a drywall joint, but it is a problem for the person applying the trim. One way to attack the problem is to use a *surform tool* to shave down the built-up drywall compound. The surform has an expanded metal blade that is held in a frame so that it can be used like a rasp or plane.

Although you cannot sharpen files and rasps, you can, and should, keep them clean. The tool for this job is called a file card. Use the card like a brush to remove any built-up debris from file and rasp teeth.

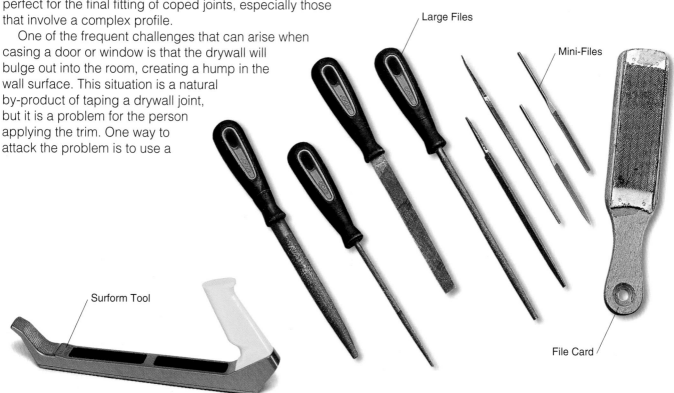

Large Files

Mini-Files

Surform Tool

File Card

Pry Bars, Pliers, and Nippers

Trim carpentry is often a game of finesse. Many jobs require careful and patient fitting and re-fitting in order to achieve a tight fit between two parts. In that pursuit, many different tools can be brought into the mix, but some of the most effective, and necessary, are listed below.

When you need to remove an old molding, or coax a new piece into position, a *pry bar* is the tool for the job. These come in a wide variety of configurations, but the most useful for trim are the versions with flat ends, appropriately called flat bars. You will find some bars as short as 4 inches and some longer than 24 inches. If you select two different styles, usually those on the smaller side, you will be set for most jobs. In addition, it's useful to have a few different *putty knives* handy for scraping, gentle prying, and filling nailholes.

If your project includes removal of existing molding, you will need a way to remove the old nails from that stock. Two great tools for the job are *end nippers* and *locking pliers*. If you were to hammer the nails back through the face side, there is a great risk of chipping the material. With either of these tools, you can grab the protruding end of the nail and pull it through the back side of the board. This technique maintains the face side of the molding, allowing you to reuse it.

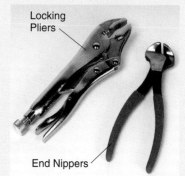

Locking Pliers

End Nippers

Work-Holding Tools

When you get involved in almost any wood-cutting or shaping process, the issue of how to hold the workpiece will arise. You simply cannot do most woodworking operations safely and accurately if you are crouched on the living room floor. Of course, you can always hijack the kitchen or dining room table, but that's not always a popular, or practical, approach. The alternative solutions you can devise are endless, but some basic options will cover most situations.

Saw Horses. *Saw horses* are a simple and flexible support system for all types of work. You will find commercial models in steel and plastic, and you can always make your own from wood. Just about any horses that you buy will fold up for compact storage, and that can be a compelling reason to go the commercial route. Look for models that are sturdy and that will hold your work and tools at a comfortable height.

Clamping Worktables. Several manufacturers offer a folding worktable with moveable top panels that function as a vise for holding work. These tables provide an ample top surface that can hold a miter saw firmly between its clamping dogs and can also provide work-holding power for planing, sawing, routing, or chiseling. Their portability lets you take the worktable to the work site.

Clamps. The variety in styles and sizes of *clamps* is vast. And it is a traditional woodworker's refrain that "you can never have enough clamps." Clamps are used to hold a joint together while glue sets or while you drive a mechanical fastener. But they are also handy, when you do not have access to a workbench and vise, for stabilizing a board for sawing or planing. Small clamps are great for temporarily holding a molding in place or positioning a stop for repeat cuts on the miter saw. For a beginning tool kit, start with two or three of each of these types: spring clamps, C-clamps, lightweight bar clamps, and quick-release clamps. You will soon learn which type is most useful for your style of work.

Adjustable Clamping Worktable

Clamping Dog

Holding tools are like having an extra set of hands. The clamping worktable, above, and a vise, left, can help make a number of jobs go easier.

Vises. If you have the luxury of having a dedicated workbench, one of the nicest modifications you can make is to add a *vise*. Vises for woodworking are available in many sizes, configurations, and prices. For most trim jobs, a lightweight vise that clamps to the top of a worktable will be sufficient. Whatever type you select, make sure that it has a provision for lining the jaws with wood so that you do not mar your workpieces when holding them.

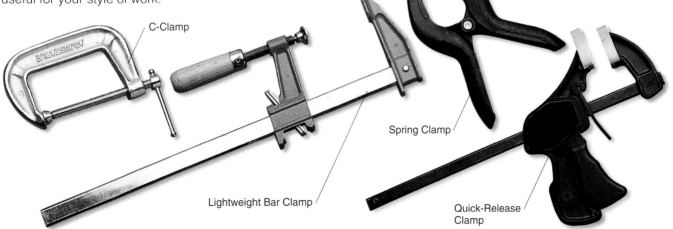

C-Clamp

Spring Clamp

Lightweight Bar Clamp

Quick-Release Clamp

Installation Tools

Hammers. The *hammer* is the most basic of hand tools—and probably the oldest. Primitive humans used some sort of hammering device at the dawn of civilization, but it is still a valued tool in the carpenter's tool kit. Although the popular image of hammer use in our culture is a rather crude one, in experienced hands a hammer can be a precise and subtle tool. For trimwork, look for a 16-ounce claw hammer. You will find models with curved and straight claws. Some "experts" will suggest that the curved claw model is preferred for trim; in fact, either style will be fine. Materials for the shaft include wood, fiberglass, and steel and, once again, personal preference rules. Of course, each manufacturer will offer their version of the "best" hammer, but you should choose one that feels comfortable and seems well balanced. If at all possible, test the hammer by driving some nails before purchasing it.

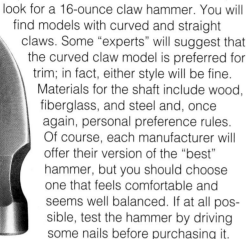

Curved Claw

Straight Claw

Nail Sets. A *nail set* is a hardened steel tool with a tapered end that is used to drive a finishing nail below a wood surface. Sets come in various sizes to correspond to different size nail heads. To avoid hammer marks, drive the nail to within ⅛ inch of the surface and finish the job using the nail set. Make sure you use the appropriately sized set, or it could slip off the head and damage the wood.

Power Drills and Screwdrivers. These are tools that you will reach for frequently on most trim projects. You will use these to drill pilot holes for nails and screws, to drive screws for installing hardware or drywall, and to assemble jamb sets. This is a case where cordless models are certainly a worthwhile investment. Most tool companies offer combination drill/drivers with adjustable clutch settings. These can operate at high or low speeds, and you can set the torque for any job requirement—high for drilling in wood or low for driving small screws. You will find models rated from 7.2 to 24 volts, but as a nonprofessional, if you select a 12- or 14.4-volt unit, you will have plenty of drilling power. An additional attraction of the cordless models is that they all come with keyless chucks, so you don't have to worry about keeping track of the chuck key.

Cordless Drill and Charger

Finishing Nailer

Brad Nailer

Nail Clips

Compressor

In addition to having a power driver, you'll want to have an assortment of hand drivers, because there will always be those jobs where a power tool is too large or awkward. Try to include at least two sizes of driver in each common screw category: flat blade, Phillips, and Robertson (square drive).

Power Nailers

If your plans include extensive trim-work, the advantages of a *pneumatic nail gun* are obvious—increased speed and no hammer marks. But, even for a small job, there are reasons to consider a nail gun. First, the nails used in a finishing nail gun are thinner than those you drive by hand, so there is less chance of splitting the wood when nailing near an edge. You can adjust the pneumatic pressure that drives the gun, so with a simple pull of the trigger, you can drive and set the nail below the wood surface. When working with hardwood molding, you need to drill pilot holes for nails that will be driven by hand, but a pneumatic gun will shoot them home in one step.

Compressors. To drive a pneumatic nail gun, you need a *compressor*. Look for an electric model in the range of 1.5–2.5 horsepower. These are available in designs that are either oil-lubricated or oil-less, and for occasional use in applying trim, either style will be fine. Get an air hose that is at least 25 feet long, or you will find yourself moving the compressor every few minutes.

Using a Nail Gun

The ability to drive and set a nail in one step can save much time and effort even when applying trim to a small room. Look for a gun that will accept nails up to 2½ inches long. For fine work, a brad gun will shoot shorter and thinner fasteners. These tools are widely available from rental agencies, so you do not need to purchase one for a small job.

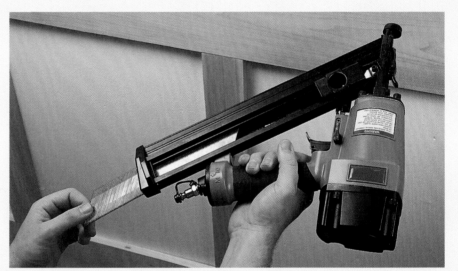

1 Pneumatic nailers use long clips of glued-together nails for easy loading. Use thin beads for finish work.

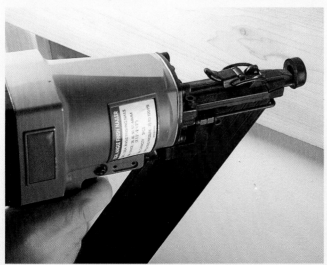

2 For best results, make sure the firing head is perpendicular to the work surface.

3 For safety, most pneumatic nailers won't fire unless the tip is pressed firmly against the work.

doors & windows

Common Joinery for Window & Door Trim

The wood trim around windows and doors is called casing, and it can be installed in all sorts of ways to accentuate a particular decorative style.

Generally, the style of the trim (and the joinery used to install it) will be consistent throughout a house. There's no reason, however, not to explore variations on whatever style you choose. In a study, for example, you might want to make the casing more ornate in order to complement other woodwork in the room. In a laundry room you might opt for the simplest casing to save money. Nearly all casing installations, however, will use some version of two joints: the miter and the butt. You will never need to cut a coped joint on casing.

Common Joinery for Windows and Doors

A miter joint is most often used where the side casing joins the head casing. At the sill (on windows) or at the floor (on doors), a butt joint is most common.

Miter Joints • **Window** • **Molded Trim** • **Butt Joints**

Miter Joints • **Door** • **Molded Trim** • **Butt Joints**

Butt Joints • **Window** • **Flat Trim** • **Butt Joints**

Corner Blocks • **Door** • **Butt Joints**

Casing Styles

In most homes, you will find mitered casing around the windows and doors. This type of casing joinery goes up quickly and is a part of every carpenter's skills. But you can use other styles. One of the hallmarks of traditional detailing is the extra care and effort spent upon it.

The casing of a door generally follows the style of any window casing in the same room. When designing the trim detailing for any room, therefore, make sure that you consider casing that will look good both on windows and on doors.

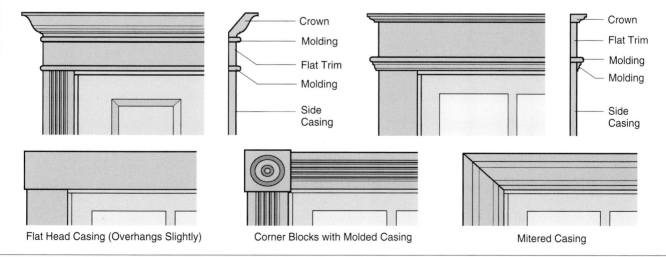

Crown — Molding — Flat Trim — Molding — Side Casing

Crown — Flat Trim — Molding — Molding — Side Casing

Flat Head Casing (Overhangs Slightly)

Corner Blocks with Molded Casing

Mitered Casing

Prehung Doors

If you want to add a door to a room, selecting a prehung door can make the installation simple and quick. With a prehung door, you eliminate the need to fit the door to the opening, to cut mortises for the hinges and lockset, and to fit the door stops.

All of the really fussy and time-consuming work is already done for you, and for the beginner or pro, this can be a real advantage.

Most lumberyards and home centers carry a variety of door styles for prehung applications. In addition, you can often choose between pine jambs that can be painted or stained,

or hardwood jambs, with red oak being the most common choice. Interior doors can have a flush design—with a flat veneered or fiberboard surface—solid wood panels, or molded fiberboard panels. Of course, it is also possible to custom order a more unusual combination of door and jamb and have it prehung for you.

Installing a Prehung Door

1. Use a nail set or punch to loosen the hinge pins on your prehung door. Lift the pins from the hinges, and gently pull the door free from the jamb assembly.

2. Stand the jamb assembly in the door opening with both side jambs resting on the floor. Use a 24-in. level to check that the head jamb is level in the opening.

3. If necessary, place shims beneath one of the side jambs to bring the head level. Measure the height of the shim; then mark the bottom of the opposite jamb to remove that same amount.

4. Cut the bottom of the high side jamb along your layout mark. A small Japanese Ryoba saw is an excellent tool for the job, but you can use any saw that is handy.

5. Use a long, straight 2x4 and 4-ft. level to check that the jack stud on the hinge side of the door is plumb—if it is not, you will need to place shims between the jamb and stud.

6. Use 8d or 10d finishing nails to fasten the hinge jamb to the jack stud. Place two nails near the top of the jamb; then check that the edge of the jamb is plumb before nailing the rest of the jamb.

7. Use a flat bar to pry the jamb out, and slide tapered shims behind the jamb. Be sure to use two shims, one driven from each side, to keep the jamb square. Use shims every 16 in.

8. Re-hang the door, and use it as a guide in adjusting the latch jamb. Place shims between the jamb and jack stud to maintain a uniform gap between the door edge and jamb.

9. Use a sharp utility knife to score the shims at the point where they protrude beyond the wall surface. After scoring the shim, you should be able to snap it off easily.

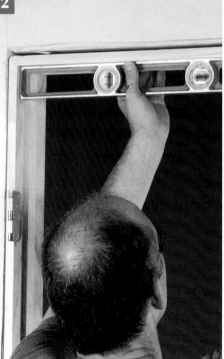

When ordering a door, you will not only need to specify the style, material, and size, but also the direction you wish the door to open. The convention that applies to this issue is as follows: if you open the door toward you and the hinges are on the right side, the door is a right-handed door; if the hinges are on the left when it opens toward you, it is a left-handed door.

The width of a standard prehung door jamb used with typical 2x4 wall framing is 4⁹⁄₁₆ inches, which allows the door jamb to just barely protrude beyond the drywall surface. This compensates for small irregularities in wall thickness.

Installing Prehung Doors

To begin your installation, remove the door from the frame by knocking out the hinge pins. You can use a nail set or punch to drive the pins out. Stand the frame in the opening, and check that the head jamb is level. If one side is higher than the other, block up the low side until it is correct; then note the thickness of the blocking required. Mark the bottom of the high side jamb to remove that same amount, and cut it with a circular saw, jig saw, or handsaw.

Test the Frame. Place the frame in the opening again to make sure that the head is level. Next, check to see if the jack stud on the hinge side of the door is plumb. If it is, use 8d or 10d finishing nails to nail the top of the jamb to the stud; then place the level on the edge of the jamb to make sure that it is plumb in both directions. Adjust the jamb as necessary, and nail the bottom. Position the nails near the top, bottom, and center of the jamb.

Out-of-Plumb Jack Stud. If the jack stud is not plumb, use a flat bar to pry the jamb away from the stud, and slip tapered shims behind the jamb to hold it in position. To keep the jamb straight, place shims, in pairs, about every 16 inches along the length of the jamb. Drive nails just below each pair of shims to keep them in place. Once the hinge jamb is nailed, rehang the door and use it as a guide in positioning the opposite jamb. Place shims between the jamb and opposite jack stud to achieve a uniform gap between the door and jamb. Again, position nails just under the shims.

Test the operation of the door to make sure that it opens and closes properly. Examine the fit of the stop against the closed door. There should be no gaps at the swinging side and a uniform gap of ¹⁄₁₆ inch or less on the hinge side, so the door does not bind. Finally, use a sharp utility knife to score the shims flush to the jamb, and snap off the protruding ends.

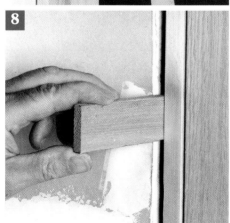

1. Cut the head jamb to length, and mark the joint outline with a square for a ¾-in. jamb leg.

2. Set the blade depth on a circular saw to reach halfway (⅜ in.) through the thickness of the board.

3. To control the rabbet cut, firmly clamp a guide board and the jamb to a stable bench.

4. Make the innermost cut with the saw along the guide. Then make multiple passes to kerf the remaining wood.

5. You can use the saw to remove all the wood, or clean up the thin strips between kerfs using a sharp chisel.

6. When the rabbet is cleaned up and ready for assembly, mark a nailing line on the outside of the joint.

7. Add glue to the mating surfaces of the jamb parts just prior to assembling them.

8. Square up the jamb frame before fastening. You may want to set the pieces around a square block for support.

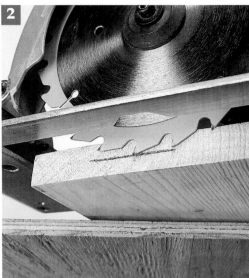

Assembling a Jamb

Many newer homes feature drywall jambs in passageways between rooms, but it is not difficult to add a wooden jamb and casing to the opening. The first step is to engage in some demolition work. In drywall openings, a metal corner bead is applied to the corners to form a straight, neat edge. As a result, these corners tend to flare out, and they are thicker than the rest of the wall—a potential problem when applying casing.

Expose the Corner Bead. Beginning at the bottom of the wall, use a flat pry bar to expose the corner bead and pry it away from the wall. Most beads are installed with 1¼-inch drywall nails and will come away easily. Work your way up each corner and across the top of the opening; then pry off the drywall strip that lines the inside of the opening to expose the jack studs and header. If the drywall extends into the opening, use a drywall saw to trim it flush to the inside surfaces of the studs and header.

Custom Jambs. You can certainly purchase standard jambs from a lumberyard, but it is easy to make the jambs for the opening from 1x6 pine stock. For normal wall construction, rip jamb stock to a width of 4⁹⁄₁₆ inches. It's always a good idea to check the thickness of the wall to see if there is variation in the measurement. Adjust your jamb width as required, allowing ¹⁄₁₆ inch more than the overall wall thickness. Next, measure the width of the rough opening in several places along the jack studs. Take the smallest measurement and subtract 1¼ inches to arrive at the length of the head jamb. Cut the side jambs about ¼ inch shorter than the rough opening height.

Use the router and edge guide, or a circular saw, to cut a ⅜-inch-deep by ¾-inch-wide rabbet across the top of each side jamb. Fasten the side jambs to the head jamb with screws or nails and glue. If you use screws, drill and counterbore pilot holes in the side jambs and small pilot holes into the end-grain of the head jamb to avoid splitting the stock. To simplify installation, tack a scrap board across the bottom edges of the side jambs to hold the parts square.

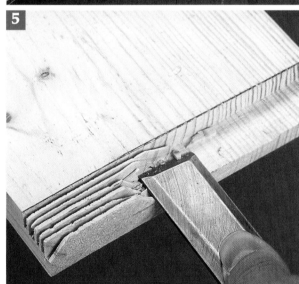

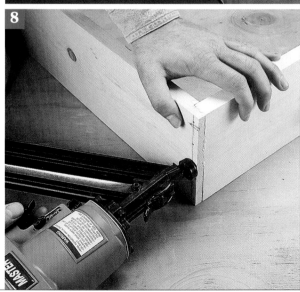

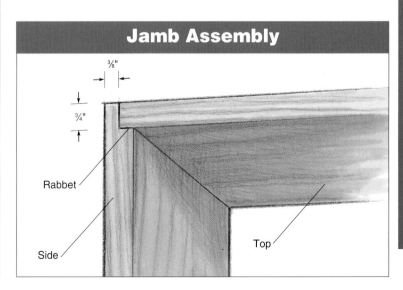

Jamb Assembly

⅜"

¾"

Rabbet

Side

Top

Installing Simple Colonial Casings

1. Mark the reveal by sliding the blade on the combination square. Cut a miter on one end of the casing.

2. Align the short side of the miter with one reveal mark; transfer the opposite mark to the casing.

3. Use 4d finishing nails to tack the head casing to the head jamb of the door. Leave the nailheads exposed.

4. Cut a miter on a piece of side casing. Rest the miter on the floor or spacer (for carpet or finished floor).

5. Mark the length of the side casing pieces by running a pencil along the top edge of the head casing.

6. Apply a small bead of glue to both miter surfaces. Nail the side casing to the jamb and wall framing.

7. Drive a 4d finishing nail through the edge of the casing to lock the miter joint together.

8. Use a nail set to recess the nailheads about ⅛ in. below the wood surface.

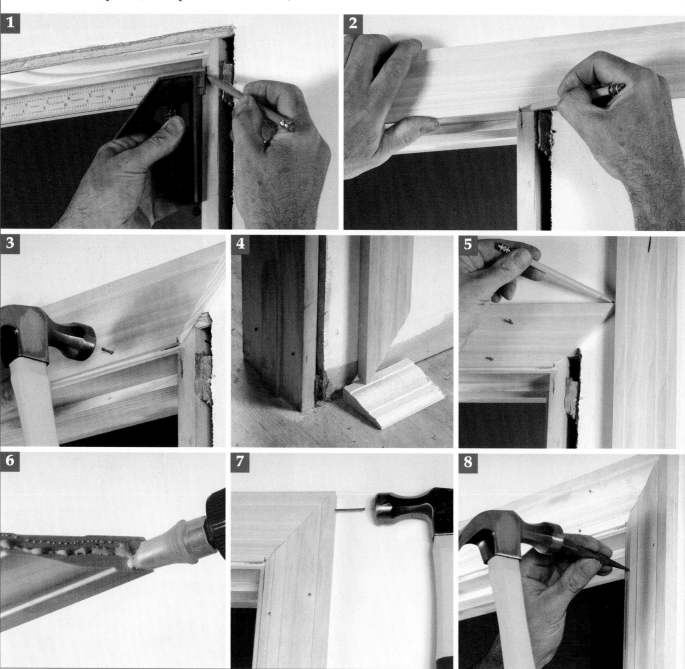

Door Casings

Some casing styles feature mitered corners at the joints of the side and head casing; other styles use butt joints; and there are certain treatments that layer a mitered molding over butt-jointed flat stock. All styles, however, have one element in common, and that is called a reveal. Instead of fastening the casing flush with the door side of the jamb, it is traditional to hold it back to allow a small, uniform margin of jamb to be exposed on its edge. The setback is known as the reveal, and this treatment applies to window casing and door casing alike. The actual dimension of the reveal you use is up to you, but 1/8 to 5/32 inch is typical. If the reveal is too large, you reduce the amount of jamb available for nailing the casing, and if it is too small, even the smallest discrepancy becomes visible. Whatever measurement you decide to use, it is important that you make it the standard for the entire job so that you maintain a uniform look throughout. Use a combination square as a gauge, and place light pencil marks at the corners, center, and ends of your jambs to indicate the amount of setback.

Evaluate the Condition of the Door

Begin by making sure that the head and side jambs are level and plumb. When you check the side jambs, use a long straightedge with the level to span the entire jamb length. Then use a framing square to check the head and side jambs. If you find that the corners are not square, use a sliding bevel gauge to determine the actual angle. Transfer the angle to a piece of scrap lumber or cardboard; then use an angle gauge to measure the angle. Use one-half of that angle for your miter saw setting to cut the corner joint.

Simple Colonial Casing

The one-piece "Colonial" casing is one of the simplest treatments for door and window casing. Along with the "clamshell" or "ranch" molding, it is one of the standard choices for homebuilders throughout the country. The techniques for either type are essentially the same.

In a mitered casing installation, the desired result is a continuous and seamless border of molding around the door opening. Begin by laying out the jamb reveals at the top corners, bottom, and midpoint of the jamb. Next, cut a miter on one end of the head casing stock and hold it in place, aligning the short end of the miter with one of the reveal marks on the side casing. Use a sharp pencil to mark the short point of the opposite miter on the other end of the molding.

Attach the Head Casing. Cut the piece to length, and tack it in place by driving 4d finishing nails driven into the edge of the jamb and 6d or 8d finishing nails into the wall framing—leave the nailheads protruding at this point in case you need to remove the part for adjustment.

Cut the matching miter angles on the side casing pieces, but leave them a few inches long. Instead of measuring the side casing pieces, it is easier, and more accurate, to directly transfer the length onto the stock. Simply invert one of the pieces of side casing so that the long point of the miter rests on the floor and the outside edge of the casing rests against the long point of the head casing. Mark the length of the casing, and make the square cut. If you need to make allowance for carpet or finish flooring, simply place an appropriate spacer under the point of the casing.

Attach Side Casing. Once the casing is cut to length, spread some carpenter's glue on the mating surfaces of the miter joint, and tack the casing in place. Drive 4d finishing nails into the edge of the jamb and 6d or 8d finishing nails to fasten the casing to the framing under the wall surface. Space the pairs of nails about 16 inches apart. Check that the miters are nice and tight; then drive a 4d finishing nail through the edge of the casing to lock the joint together. Set the nailheads below the wood surface.

TRIM TIP

Mark Once. As a general rule, you are always better off directly marking the size of a trim piece than measuring its length. Whenever you measure and mark a piece for length, there is an inevitable degree of variation in the way the dimension is transferred to the work piece. By marking the size of a piece directly in its ultimate location, you reduce the opportunity for careless errors.

Built-Up Colonial Casing

Factory-made Colonial casing is designed to mimic the more elaborate forms of a traditionally installed, built-up casing. Using readily available stock, you can create a larger and more detailed casing that conveys a more nuanced sense of style than is available with an off-the-shelf profile. The process is not difficult; it uses 1x4 and 1x2 boards, and stock panel or base cap molding. 1x4 boards form the foundation of the casing. While you can certainly leave the edges of the boards square, or ease them gently with sandpaper, the casing will be more interesting if you add a molded profile to the inside edge. In order to do this, install an ogee or cove bit in the router, and use it to cut the profile along one edge of each 1x4 board.

Cut the Head Casing. First, mark the reveals on the jamb edges. Then cut a piece of 1x4 to length for the head casing with an appropriate miter cut on each end. Although it is not technically necessary to create a glue joint between the side and head casings, it is good trim practice when dealing with wide, flat stock.

Installing Built-Up Colonial Casings

1. A router with an edge-profiling bit makes quick work of molding the edges of casing stock. Clamp the casing blank to the worktable before beginning the cut. You can also mount the router in a router table.

2. Cut appropriate miters for the corner joints. Mark the center of each joining plate slot on the face of the casing; then clamp a piece to the worktable to cut the slot. Hold the plate jointer and stock tightly on the table.

3. Tack the head casing to the head jamb with 4d finish-ing nails; then spread glue on the miter surfaces, in both slots, and on the joining plate. Insert the plate in one side of the joint, and assemble the joint.

4. Cut backband strips to size with appropriate bevels for the corner joints. Use 6d finishing nails, or a nail gun, to fasten the strips to the outside edges of the casing.

5. Cut panel molding to fit tightly inside the backband border. Nail the molding to the casing with 4d finishing nails.

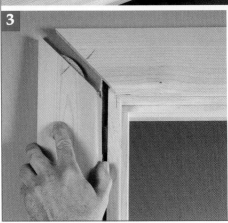

Tight Connections. Another useful technique is to use a joining plate in the joint between the two casing parts. The joining plate serves two functions. First, it strengthens the joint, and second, it keeps the faces of the adjoining parts perfectly aligned. Mark the location of the center of each slot on the top surface of the head casing and cut the slots. Then tack the head casing in position over the door opening. Trim the side casings to size; cut the matching plate slots; and install those, applying glue to the slots and joining plates before nailing the parts in place.

Installing the Backband. Cut 1x2 stock to wrap around the outside edges of the flat casing—this treatment is known as a backband. Notice that the cuts at the corner joints need to be 45-degree bevels, rather than flat miters. Install the backband to the outside edges of the flat casing using 6d finishing nails. Begin with the head casing, and then move to the sides. Finally, cut the panel or base cap molding to size so that its outside edge sits tight to the inside face of the backband. Install it using 4d finishing nails.

Create a custom design by adding a simple backband and some panel molding to flat Colonial casing.

TRIM TIP

Closing Gaps. When dealing with wide casing, it is pretty common to require a bit of adjustment to get the miters to close tightly. If the doorjamb protrudes beyond the wall surface even $\frac{1}{16}$ inch you may have difficulty closing the miter joint. In this case, you can place shims behind the outer edges of the casing to create a tight joint. Score the shims with a sharp knife, and snap off the protruding portion. The backband will cover the gap between the casing and wall.

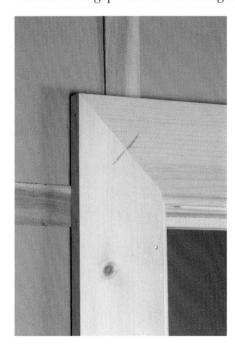

Use shims to help the miter joints close tightly. Score and remove the protruding section of the shims.

Built-up moldings add texture and design interest to the casings around doorways, doors, and windows.

Traditional-Style Casing

In the period from the 1920s through the 1940s, many homes were built in a style that is often called "traditional." These homes predate the use of the "ranch" and "colonial" casings that are so frequently used today. Door and window openings featured wide, flat casings with a simple backband. This treatment creates a nice framework for these room openings and is definitely worth considering. One of the nice features of this trim detail is that the flat casing stock is joined at the head with a simple butt joint. This eliminates the need for fussing with a miter joint on wide stock.

Lay Out the Casing. To determine the length of the head casing, measure the distance between the reveal marks on the side casing, and add twice the width of a piece of side casing—for 3½-inch-wide stock you would add 7 inches. Lay out and cut the joining plate slots in the bottom edge of the head casing. Cut the side casings to length; cut matching slots in the top end of each piece. Tack the side casings to the door jamb; then apply glue to the joining plate slots and plates. Install the plates to the top of each side casing; slip the head casing into position; and nail it to the head jamb. If necessary, slip tapered shims behind the outer edge of the casing stock to ensure that the joints between side and head casing are flush.

Installing Traditional-Style Casings

1. Mark the locations of joining plate slots in the bottom edge of the head casing; then use the plate joiner to cut the slots.

2. Cut plate slots in the top ends of side casings. To avoid kickback when cutting into end grain, clamp the stock to the table, and use two hands to control the plate joiner.

3. Use 4d or 6d finishing nails to fasten the side casing to the edge of the doorjamb. Wait until the head casing is in place to nail the outer edge to the wall.

4. Spread glue in the plate slots and on the joining plates; then assemble the head/side casing joints. Nail the head casing to the head jamb; then nail the outer edge of the casing.

5. Cut the backband strips to size with appropriately beveled ends. Use 6d finishing nails to fasten the bands to the outer edge of the casing.

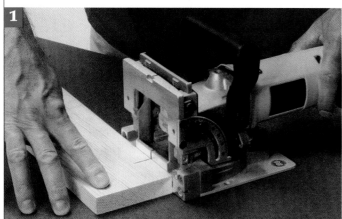

Cut the Backband. Measure and cut the backband stock to length with appropriately beveled ends. There are many situations where a wall surface is so irregular that gaps inevitably occur between the casing and wall. On jobs that will be painted, you can always apply a small bead of caulk to fill any gaps. But on a job that will receive a clear finish, caulk is not an option. This is a situation where the backband can be planed to fit tightly to the wall surface. (See "Scribing a Backband to the Wall," below.)

Many home centers stock a backband molding that is cut in an "L"-shaped cross section, so that it wraps around the outside edge of the casing instead of just butting to it. These products are viable alternatives for your door trim; just do not feel that their offerings are your only options.

Simple butt joints are the distinguishing characteristics of traditional-style casing. The addition of a backband creates an elegant design.

Scribing a Backband to the Wall

If you notice that there are gaps between the wall and backband, it's a simple matter to scribe it to fit. Scribing involves marking the stock to match the wall profile and then removing material from the areas adjacent to the high points so that the molding can sit tight to the wall along its entire length.

Begin by applying a strip of masking tape to the outer surface of the backband. The tape will allow you to better see the scribed pencil lines. Next, hold the molding against the wall, in position, and set your scribers to a width that matches the widest gap between the wall and molding. Hold the two wings of the scriber parallel with the floor as you trace the wall profile onto the taped surface of the molding.

Remove the backband to a work surface, and use a sharp block plane to remove material until the pencil line is left exposed. Test the fit of the piece, and make any necessary adjustments.

If you remove stock from the top edges of a side backband, the top band will also need to be adjusted so that it does not protrude beyond the sides. If the top piece is already installed, it is a simple matter to plane the face to the required depth.

1 Apply masking tape to the outside edge of the backband; hold the band against the wall; and use scribers to mark the required adjustment.

2 Use a sharp block plane to trim the backband to fit the wall profile. Plane just up to the scribed line. Test the fit, and adjust if necessary.

Window Trim

Some aspects of window trim are identical to those on door trim. Casing details, once established for any particular job, are applied equally to both types of opening. However, there are some features of each that are particular. Of course, plinth blocks are only relevant in a discussion of door casing. In similar fashion, window stools, aprons, and extension jambs are particular to window trim. And there is a specific treatment that is an option with windows that does not apply to door openings, and that is the picture-frame casing—casing that surrounds all four sides of the opening.

Before you start to apply trim to a window, you should take a few minutes in preparation. As part of most window installations, shims are placed between the jambs and rough framing to help maintain the position of the unit. Check each of these shims to make sure that they are firmly lodged in place, with nails driven either through the shim or in very close proximity. Make sure that no shims protrude beyond the wall surface. Use a sharp utility knife to score any shim that is too long, and snap off the

Adding Extension Jambs

1. Use a straightedge and ruler to measure the depth of required extension jambs. Check the measurements at several places around the frame, and use the largest dimension.

2. If extension jambs are wider than 1¼ in., it is best to assemble them into a frame before installing them to the window. Drill and countersink pilot holes, and screw the parts together.

3. If there is no insulation around a window, use non-

expanding foam to fill any gaps before installing the extension jambs. Cut off any excess after the foam sets.

4. Place the extension jamb assembly into the window opening, and align the inside surfaces with the factory window jambs.

5. Use trim screws to fasten the extension jamb assembly to the factory window jambs. If you center the screws in the edge of the jambs, the holes will be covered by the casing.

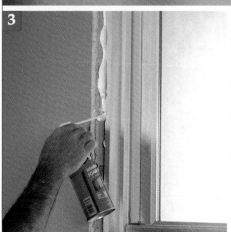

Once you determine the width of the extensions, use a table saw to rip them to width. If at all possible, maintain one factory edge on each jamb to minimize edge preparation, and mount that edge facing into the room. Jambs that are less than 1¼ inches wide can be nailed directly to the factory jambs; just drill pilot holes through the stock to keep the nails going straight, and to avoid splitting. If the extensions need to be wider than 1¼ inch, it is best to assemble them into a frame and then use long trim-head screws to fasten the entire assembly to the window. If you are concerned about keeping the extensions perfectly flush to the factory jambs, you have the option of creating a small reveal between the parts.

Troubleshooting. Sometimes, the distance varies between the factory jambs and wall surface at different spots around the perimeter of the window. If the difference is small, less than ⅛-inch, pick the greatest measurement and cut all extensions to that dimension. You can take up that discrepancy with shims and caulk or by skim-coating the wall surface. If the difference in dimension is great, you can plane the strips to follow the wall surface.

excess. Many installers stuff fiberglass insulation in the space between the window and framing. This practice is fine as long as the insulation is not overly compressed, which will cause it to become ineffective. As an alternative, you can purchase a can of nonexpanding foam insulation and use it to fill the spaces around the window. If you use the foam, first pry out any fiberglass insulation so the foam can completely fill the cavity.

Extension Jambs

To prepare a window for casing, the first step is to determine whether you will require extension jambs. Because exterior walls are framed at different thicknesses and receive different interior wall treatments, the finished depth of an exterior wall can vary considerably from job to job. Instead of offering windows with different jamb widths, most manufacturers rely on the trim carpenter to adapt the windows to the site by applying extension jambs to the window. Some window companies offer proprietary extension jamb stock that has an interlocking profile, but most allow for site-built extensions; most often ¾-inch clear pine is used, but hardwood extensions could also work.

Establish the Extension Size. Use a small straightedge to measure the distance between the edge of the jambs and the wall surface. Sometimes a window is installed so that it is not perfectly parallel with the wall surface, so check the dimensions at several spots around the window frame, and use the largest measurement. Ideally, the jambs should be about ¹⁄₁₆-inch proud of the wall.

Window casings can follow a traditional style or be totally unique.

Stool and Apron

The traditional approach to window trim involves the installation of a wide, horizontal shelf-like member at the bottom of the window. Many people mistakenly refer to this piece as a window sill; however, the correct term is window stool. (Sill refers to the angled exterior portion of the window designed to shed water and snow.) Stools are generally cut from 5/4 stock. You can sometimes purchase dedicated stool stock from a millwork supplier; this material will usually have a molded profile along its front edge, and sometimes an angled rabbet that is designed to sit over the sloped window sill.

However, it is a simple matter to fabricate your own stool stock, either with or without a molded edge, from 5/4 lumber. The stool extends past the window jambs onto the wall surface—these extensions are known as horns. The horns support the side casings, and generally extend about 3/4 inch beyond the casing on both end and face. The gap between the wall surface and the bottom of the stool is covered by a trim piece called an apron.

Add Extensions. If extension jambs are necessary, install them first. Older windows require extensions only on the top and sides as the stool could rest directly on the interior portion of the sill. On newer windows, it is often appropriate to install extension jambs on all four sides of the window—even when a stool will be used. On these windows, the sill only extends to the exterior portion of the window, so the bottom extension provides support for the stool and eliminates the need for separate blocking.

Casing Reveals. Once the extension jambs are in place, lay out the casing reveals. Gauge the eventual position of the outside edge of the side casing by taking a piece of casing stock and holding it on the reveal mark. Place a light mark on the wall surface to indicate the outside edge of the casing; then place another mark 3/4 inch outside that line to indicate the end of the stool. Repeat this process on the opposite side of the window. Measure the distance between those marks on either side of the window to arrive at the overall stool width; then crosscut the stock to length.

Lay Out the Horns. Hold the stool blank against the wall with its ends on the outside gauge marks. Use a square and sharp pencil to mark the locations of the inside surfaces of window jambs on the stool. Then measure the distance between the stool and the window sash. In some cases, the distance may be different at each end of the sash. In these situations, use the larger measurement, and plane the leading edge of the stool to fit later.

The ends of the stool that project beyond the sides of the window and onto the wall surface are called the horns. Use a square to extend your measurement marks onto the stool surface to indicate the cuts for the horns.

Calculate the overall depth of the stool by adding the casing thickness plus 3/4 inch to the horn layout line.

Trim the Horn. Use the table saw to rip the stool to the desired width. Next, use a hand saw or jig saw to make the cutouts for the horns. Test the fit of the stool in the opening. On some windows, you will need to make further notches and rabbet cuts to accommodate window stop and specialized weather-stripping. The horns of the stool should sit tight to the wall surface and there should be a uniform gap between the sash and the stool of about 1/32 inch. You can easily gauge the gap by slipping a piece of cardboard between the sash and stool. Use a sharp block plane to adjust the fit of the stool against the sash.

The horns of a window stool extend beyond the casing.

1. Align a piece of casing with the reveal mark on the window jambs, and mark its outside edge on the wall. Place another mark ¾ in. away to indicate the end of the window stool.

2. Hold the stool stock in place against the window, and use a square and sharp pencil to mark the inside dimensions of the window jambs onto the stool surface.

3. Use a combination square to gauge the depth of the notch for the horns on the window stool.

4. Hold the body of the combination square against the edge of window stool stock; then run a pencil along the end of the blade to lay out the cutout for the stool horns.

5. Place a piece of casing stock along the horn cutout line, and lightly mark along its front face. Add ¾ in. to this dimension to determine the overall width of the window stool.

6. Use a saber saw or handsaw to cut the notches at both ends of the window stool.

7. Place the stool blank in the window opening to mark any additional notches required to fit around window stops. Some windows may require a rabbet.

8. This detail of the notch and rabbet on the edge of the window stool accommodates the jamb and a stop.

continued on page 58

3 Doors & Windows

continued from page 57

Installing a Stool and Casing

9. To avoid any binding between window sash and stool, you need to provide a gap of about $\frac{1}{32}$ in. Use cardboard to test the gap. If necessary, trim the leading edge of the stool.

10. Shape the inside edge and ends of a window stool with a router and bit of your choice. It is most common to use roundover, chamfer, or ogee profiles for this part.

11. Use 8d finishing nails to fasten the stool to the window jamb or sill. If necessary, place shims beneath the stool to keep it level.

12. Drill pilot holes through the edge of the horns before driving 8d or 10d finishing nails to fasten the stool to the wall framing.

13. For a Victorian-style casing, make a square cut on each side casing blank, and rest the cut on the stool to mark its length. It should be flush with the underside of the head jamb.

14. Place a rosette head block in place so that it overhangs the side casing evenly on each side. The inside corner of the block should be flush to the inside corner of the window jambs.

15. Cut head casing stock to length—it should fit snugly between the rosette blocks. Nail it to the head jamb and window header.

16. Cut mitered returns on the ends of apron molding stock. Apply glue to both surfaces of each miter joint before assembling the parts.

17. If necessary, use a sharp block plane to trim the top edge of the apron so that it fits tight to the stool. You can also drive nails through the stool into the top edge of the apron.

11

14

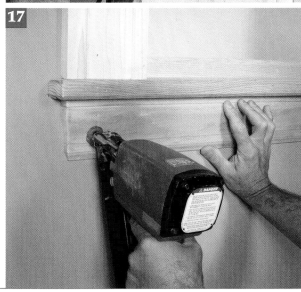

17

Shape the Edge. Use a router to shape the desired profile along the front edge and ends of the stool. It is perfectly acceptable to use a roundover, chamfer, or ogee profile for the stool. Just select a shape that works well with the casing of the windows. If you are not comfortable cutting a profile on the relatively narrow end of the stool, you can always create a mitered return to carry the profile back to the wall surface. And if you prefer a simpler treatment, just use a sanding block to ease the sharp edges of the stool.

Install the Stool. Place the stool in the opening, and install shims under it, if necessary, to adjust its position. The stool should be level, so use a spirit level to check it. Then fasten the stool to the sill or bottom jamb with 8d finishing nails. It is also a good idea to nail through the horns of the sill into the wall framing, but if you do so, be sure to first drill pilot holes for the nails.

Apply the desired casing to the sides and head jamb, following the methods discussed for door trim. The casing should rest firmly on the stool, but otherwise, the treatment is the same whether a window or door is involved.

The stock for the apron can be the same as that used for the window casing, or you can use an entirely different profile or a combination of two or more moldings. The overall length of the apron should be the same as the distance between the outside edges of the side casings—generally 1½ inches shorter than the stool. If you use flat stock for the apron, you can simply cut it to length with square cuts at the ends. If you choose profiled stock, you should cut mitered returns on the ends to continue the profile back to the wall. Hold the apron in place, and check that it fits tightly to the bottom side of the stool. If the stool is not perfectly flat or if the apron stock is not perfectly straight, it may be necessary to plane the top edge of the apron so that there is no gap between the parts. Fasten the apron to the wall using 8d finishing nails; then drive two or three nails through the stool into the top edge of the apron to lock stool and apron together.

Window Casing Assembly

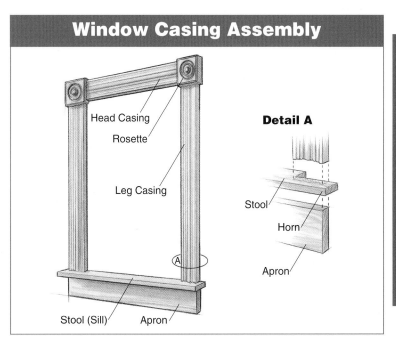

Head Casing

Rosette

Leg Casing

Detail A

Stool

Horn

Apron

Stool (Sill) Apron

Troubleshooting Casing Problems

Trimwork can be challenging when everything goes according to plan, but especially so when problems arise. Unfortunately, it is relatively rare that all parts of an installation proceed without running into something unexpected, so it's good to be prepared for those situations if need be.

Most problems with casing arise from a limited universe of causes. And although it can be tempting to lay blame on the shoulders of an errant drywall installer or previous carpenter, a problem with trim can be the result of a relatively innocent combination of small discrepancies, or oversights, that are not considered critical at that prior stage of the job. For example, a framing carpenter might reasonably assume that a small hump in wall framing would be absorbed and nullified by the drywall sheathing. Or a drywall finisher could be more concerned with creating a smooth taped joint than with the later effects of the resultant swelling in the wall surface. Of course, there is always a case when some door or window installer loses their concentration, and as a result, the jamb does not line up properly with a wall surface. Regardless of the cause, it is important to remember that trim is the place where all problems start to surface and become visible, so learn to accept those conditions as a natural part of the process.

Bulging Drywall

It is relatively common to encounter a situation where the drywall surface has a hump, or high spot, adjacent to a door opening. This can be the result of bowed framing lumber or too much joint compound. In either case, the easiest way to remedy the situation is to grind the drywall down so that it is flush to the edge of the jamb.

Smooth the Surface. First hold a piece of casing in place, and mark the location of the outside edge so you do not damage an exposed wall surface. Then use a Surform tool or other abrasive tool to abrade the drywall surface until it is flush with the jamb. Test your progress frequently with a straightedge so that you do not remove too much material. If you inadvertently damage the adjacent drywall, either lightly sand the surface or apply a skim coat of new drywall compound.

Using Filler Strips

Where a doorjamb extends beyond a wall surface, you may need to place shims between the back side of the casing and wall. Some tapered casing can be nailed to the wall, but you may have to plane a bevel on the face of the miter. Or you may have to do both.

When your casing includes a backband, the strip can often cover the gap. If no backband is used and the gap is uniform in size, you can apply a filler strip behind the casing to fill the gap. If all else fails, you can caulk or apply a thin coat of drywall compound to the wall to bring the surface flush to the edge of the jamb.

1 When a jamb protrudes beyond the wall surface. Slide filler strips between the casing and wall until the edges are flush.

2 Drive nails through both the casing and filler strips to lock them in place. A pneumatic nail gun eliminates the need to drill pilot holes.

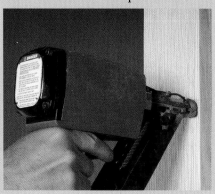

Fixing Bulging Drywall

1. Hold a piece of casing in position, and make a light pencil mark along the outside edge over the high spot. Work inside the line.

2. Use a Surform or similar abrasive tool to grind down the drywall surface until it is flush to the jamb.

Fixing Open Miter Joints

1. A jamb that protudes past the wall surface can cause an open miter joint. Be sure the joint will close by planing a back-bevel on each half of the miter.

2. If you still see a gap after installing the casing, you'll need to shim the back of the casing.

3. Carefully place shims behind the upper portion of each casing leg to help close the miter joint. Cut away the excess shims.

4. Use a good grade of latex painter's caulk to fill the gap between the back side of the casing and the wall surface.

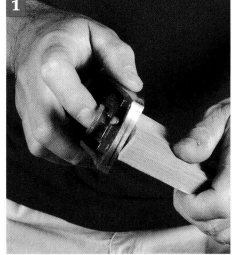

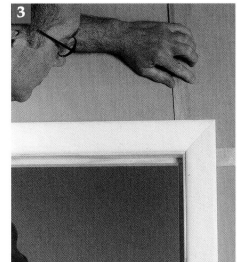

Routing a Molding Profile

The great selection of router bits provides you a means of creating your own molding profiles to personalize a trim installation. Most profile bits feature a ball-bearing pilot at the bottom of the bit, which you can use to guide the cutter along an edge. One of the advantages of cutting your own molding is that you can generate slightly different profiles with the same bit by varying the depth of the cut.

Mount the bit in the router following all manufacturer's recommendations and cautions. Adjust the appropriate depth of cut for the bit and material thickness. Clamp a small piece of scrap lumber to your worktable, and test the cut before moving on to valuable material. When you are satisfied with the profile, clamp your stock to the table and make the cut. Remember to move the router from left to right as you face the edge of the board.

If you need to cut a profile on a lot of material, you should consider using a router table for the job. Once you have set up and adjusted the router in a table, you can push the material past the cutter instead of needing to clamp each board individually. Even though your bit may have a ball-bearing pilot, always install the router table fence and align it with the face of the pilot. By using accessory hold-down jigs on the table, you can eliminate any danger of kickback as well as maintain even pressure on the stock. This will avoid burn marks and irregularities in the profile.

Narrow moldings present a different problem. Because it is difficult to use a router on narrow stock, play it safe and always rout the profile on the edge of a wide board, and then transfer the work to a circular saw or table saw to rip the molded piece off of the wide stock to the desired dimensions.

Use hold-down accessories when routing profiles on a router table.

2 Set the router on the edge of the board to see the depth of the bit. Make a test cut on scrap.

4 To work safely, clamp the board securely to a bench, and be sure the clamps are out of the router's path.

1 Select a profiling bit with a roller guide that rides along the edge of the board.

3 Adjust the depth of cut on the router. Some have a collar on the housing; others have a calibrated knob.

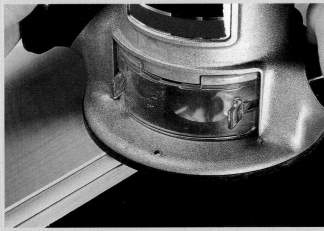

5 Make your cut pushing against the rotation of the bit, and use multiple passes to avoid chatter marks.

The best approach to selecting a casing style is to use the same design throughout the house.

Traditional-style casing is a simple but distinctive treatment for doors and windows.

base & wall trim

Base Trim

Base trim includes a variety of board and molding applications to the bottom of a wall. The trim serves a practical purpose in that it covers the inevitable gap between the wall surface and floor, but it also serves a design function in that it provides a strong visual line around the base of a room and acts as the foundation for the rest of the trim. Of course, the decision as to what type of base trim you will use is tied into the trim motif of the room as a whole. Certain base treatments are more appropriate with some trim styles than others, but a few different options provide an adequate selection for most situations. If your trim package is based on stock molding profiles, there is simple, one-piece baseboard stock available. But if you are committed to a style that features wider, more complex moldings, the base trim should be of taller, heavier stock—usually a three-piece assembly. Keep in mind that specialty millwork suppliers can offer a wide variety of base profiles that you otherwise will not find. So, to expand your options or just to be inspired, it is worth exploring these resources.

One-Piece Baseboard

Most lumberyards and home centers offer baseboard moldings in two different styles to match their stock casings—colonial and ranch (also called "clam-shell"). The height of these moldings can run from 3 to 5½ inches, and most are about ½ inch thick. Select a profile and size that is compatible with the rest of the trim details in the room. If the floor is to be carpeted, the simple baseboard is all you will require. But for a tile or hardwood floor, you should also plan to install a flexible shoe molding to cover inevitable gaps between the different materials.

Built-up Base Trim

Most traditional trim styles feature a three-piece base assembly consisting of a flat or molded baseboard, a decorative cap molding, and flexible shoe molding. Some elaborate styles add layers or embellishments to the mix, but once you understand the basic principles and techniques for the installation, you can add or subtract elements to suit your taste and the overall design.

Base Trim Height. The height of the base trim should be in proportion to the trim in the rest of the room, but it should relate to the size and height of the room, as well. A room with 8-foot-high ceilings can accept a base treatment that is 5 inches high, but a room with 9- or 10-foot ceilings needs a more substantial base—perhaps one that is 8 or 9 inches high. If you are in doubt as to the appropriate height of the molding, cut some scrap stock to various dimensions, and place it on the floor in the room to better judge the proportions.

Covering Mistakes. Even though the central portion of built-up base trim is relatively rigid, the layered construction provides a means for accommodating irregularities in both the wall and floor surfaces. Both the cap molding and shoe molding are flexible enough to conform to slight dips and humps so that most gaps can be eliminated.

Detail of one-piece baseboard with stock Colonial door casing.

Detail of three-piece base trim with traditional casing.

Plan the Installation. To make your job proceed as efficiently as possible, you should plan the order of installation of the base trim pieces. The inside corners of each base trim element need to be coped to provide tight joints, and you should minimize those situations that demand coped joints on both ends of a single piece of stock. To that end, make a simple map of each room with the order of installation noted and with the type of cut required—butt, miter, scarf, and cope. By planning ahead, your installation will go smoothly and you will end up with the neatest job possible.

If your room is to receive wall-to-wall carpet, it is customary to raise the base trim up from the subfloor about ½ inch to allow the carpet installer to tuck the ends under it. In these situations, a shoe molding is not required, as the nap of the carpet covers any gaps caused by small dips in the floor. Cut blocks of ½-inch-thick stock (small pieces of colonial or ranch base work well) to use as temporary spacers under the baseboard. Simply place them around the room, and rest the trim on them when nailing to the wall.

Base trim needs to be nailed to the wall framing. A wide baseboard is fastened with a nail driven into each wall stud and similarly spaced nails driven into the bottom plate of the wall. While typical framing dictates that there is a stud every 16 inches along a wall, this is sometimes not the case. It can save you considerable time and frustration by locating the wall studs before starting the installation. Use an electronic stud finder to scan each wall at base trim height, and make a light pencil mark on the wall or floor to indicate stud centers. If you are working with finished wall or floor surfaces, you can place a piece of masking tape on either surface to receive the pencil marks.

To avoid unnecessary marks on a finished wall surface, place a strip of masking tape on the wall just above the base trim height to mark stud locations. Use an electronic stud finder to locate framing members.

Suggested Cutting Sequences

Rectangular Room

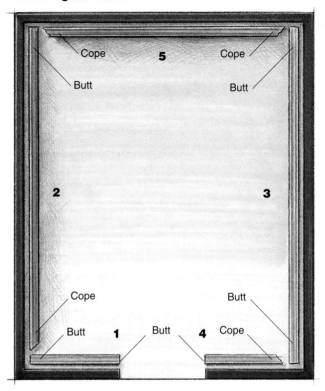

L-Shaped Room

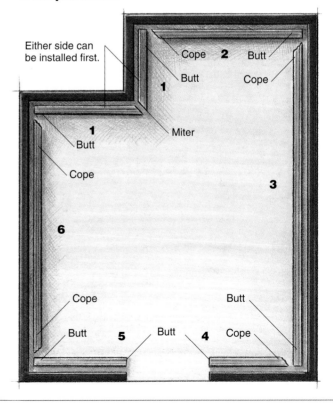

Room with Scarf Joints

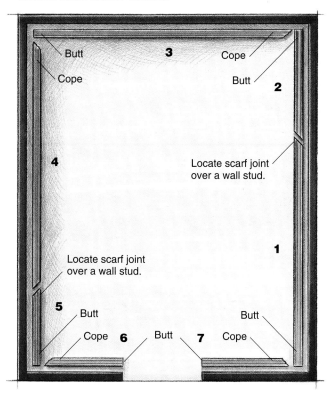

Butt · 3 · Cope

Cope · Butt · 2

4

Locate scarf joint over a wall stud.

1

Locate scarf joint over a wall stud.

5 · Butt · Butt

Cope · 6 · Butt · 7 · Cope

Room with Bay Window

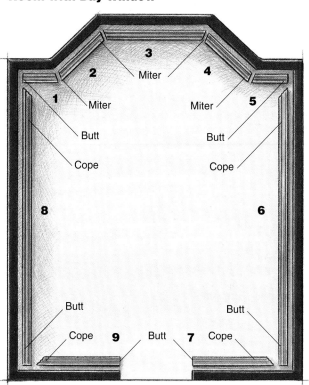

3

2 · Miter · 4

1 · Miter · Miter · 5

Butt · Butt

Cope · Cope

8 · 6

Butt · Butt

Cope · 9 · Butt · 7 · Cope

Double L-Shaped Room

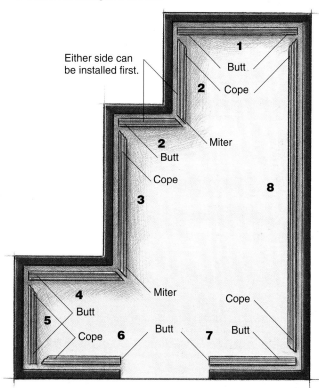

1

Either side can be installed first.

Butt

2 · Cope

Miter

2

Butt

Cope

3 · 8

Miter

4

5 · Butt

Cope · 6 · Butt · 7 · Cope · Butt

Room with Alcove

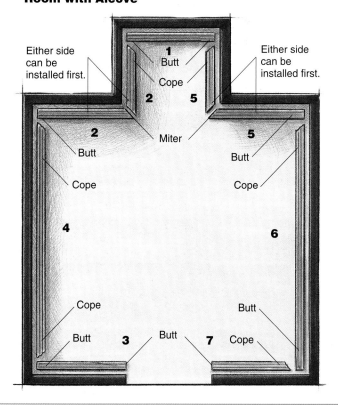

1

Either side can be installed first.

Butt

Cope

Either side can be installed first.

2 · 5

Miter

2 · 5

Butt · Butt

Cope · Cope

4 · 6

Cope · Butt

Butt · 3 · Butt · 7 · Cope

Baseboard Installation

Because a one-piece baseboard is the default approach, it makes sense to start with that type of installation. It is typical to begin with the longest closed wall in a room. Of course, there are situations where this will not be appropriate, but as a general rule this is a good approach. (See "Suggested Cutting Sequences," pages 66–67.) Professional carpenters often cut all baseboards for a room at one time, but for the amateur this can cause confusion and opens up the possibility of badly cut joints or wasted material.

The first piece of baseboard can butt squarely into the wall surface on both ends, so it is the easiest to fit. Measure the length of the wall, at baseboard height, and add 1/16 inch to that measurement. (See "Cutting Baseboard to Length," opposite.) Place the baseboard into position, and fasten it to the wall by driving a nail into each stud and one near each stud into the wall plate. If you use a pneumatic nail gun for installing the trim, the nails will automatically be set as they are driven. But if

TRIM TIP

Base Trim before Finish Flooring. A finished hardwood or tile floor can be installed either before or after the base treatment. If the base will precede the floor, use small blocks of the finished floor material as spacers under the baseboard. Place an additional layer of cardboard on top of each of these spacers to provide a small margin so that the flooring can easily slip under the wall trim. The base shoe will hide any gaps between the trimwork and the floor.

you nail by hand, you should set the nails as you finish nailing each piece of molding. If you wait until the entire room is finished to set the nails, you could cause gaps to open in some coped joints by driving one of the pieces further toward the wall surface.

Installing an Inside Corner

1. At inside corners, cut a square end on the first piece of baseboard and run it into the drywall corner. Because only the top portion of the molding will be visible, it does not need to be tight along its entire height. Note the use of a piece of finished flooring and cardboard as a spacer beneath the baseboard.

2. Cope the end of the second piece for an inside corner joint. (See "Installing Crown Molding," page 96, for tips on cutting coped joints.) Test the fit. An open joint can be the result of one of a number of factors, including a wall that is not perfectly flat or straight or a less than perfect coping job. Use a knife, rasp, file, or sandpaper to make adjustments.

3. Completed inside corner joint on one-piece baseboard. It is not unusual for a joint to require some modification to close tightly.

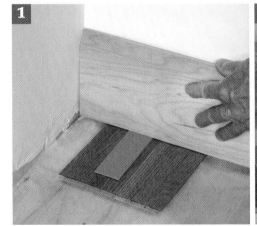

Cutting Baseboard to Length

Whenever you cut a piece of baseboard, it is a good practice to add an extra 1/16 inch to the length to ensure a tight fit and to allow you some room to adjust the joint. When fitting a piece of base between two surfaces, an extra 1/16 inch allows you to spring the molding into position, pushing the end joint closed. And when fitting an outside corner joint, the extra length gives you the opportunity to work toward a tight fit—something that does not always come automatically, especially in corners that are not perfectly square. Remember that some fitting and recutting is an expected part of trim installation.

Inside Corner Joints

A coped joint at inside corners will ensure that the molding does not separate. The technique is similar to the one used on installing crown molding shown on page 96. Cut a piece of stock to about 2 inches longer than the finished dimension for the next piece of baseboard. Use a miter saw to cut an open 45-degree bevel cut on the end that will receive the coped joint. An open bevel has its long point on the back surface of the stock, and it exposes the profile of the molded surface. Use a coping saw to cut along the exposed profile, keeping the saw blade angled to provide a back-cut or clearance angle that is slightly greater than 90 degrees.

Place the molding against the wall, and test the fit of the coped joint. If the molding is to fit against another inside wall, you will need to slightly angle the opposite end toward the center of the room to test the joint. Use a combination of knife, rasp, and file to adjust the coped profile until you have a tight fit. It is common for baseboard to be slightly tipped from a perfectly vertical plane. When this occurs, you will need to modify the coped profile to adapt to whatever situation exists. This is often a matter of making a series of small modifications until a proper fit is achieved. When satisfied, measure the length of the piece from the face of the existing molding to the opposite wall; add 1/16 inch; and cut the molding to length.

A multipiece base molding can be a strong design element in a room, yet it is easy to install. In addition, the base shoe will hide gaps between the base and the floor.

Coped inside corners help ensure that changes in humidity or building movement will not cause the trimwork to separate and show gaps at the corner.

Outside Corner Joints

On outside corners, the first step is to determine the angle of the corner. Drywall is not a precision material, and the combination of corner bead and layers of drywall compound can create corners that are either greater or less than 90 degrees. For this it is handy to have some scrap baseboard stock that you can use as test pieces. Of course, you can try to use an angle gauge to determine the angle of an outside corner, but these are usually too small to get an accurate reading.

Determine the Angle. Cut two pieces of scrap 1x6 stock, each about 18 inches long. Make a 45-degree bevel cut on the end of each piece, and test the fit of the parts on the corner. If the joint is open at the outside, slightly increase the angle of the cut; if it is open at the wall, try a slightly reduced angle. After just a few joints you will learn the amount of adjustment required to make a joint fit. Note that it is important that both pieces of a miter joint have the identical angle. Resist the temptation to cut one piece at a steeper angle than the other, as the result is that one piece of molding will protrude farther at the corner. The only remedy would then be to sand off the excess, leaving end grain visible at the joint.

Install the Molding. Once you are satisfied with the test joint, hold the molding stock against the wall, and place pencil marks on the floor (or on masking tape) to indicate the outside surface of the molding. You can then use those marks to directly scribe the long point of the miters on the base-board stock. First fit the opposite end of the baseboard to its appropriate joint and hold it in place. Keep pressure on that joint while you mark the long point of the miter on the outside corner joint; then cut the joint to the previously determined angle. Cut the second half of the mitered corner using the same technique. Nail the first piece to the wall; then apply glue to the mating surfaces of the miter joint, and use two 4d finishing nails or brads to pin the joint together. If you are nailing by hand, drill small pilot holes for the nails at the corner joint so the stock does not split—splits are much less likely when using a pneumatic nail gun. Note: for multipiece installations, record the actual angle of the outside corner so that you can use it for cutting the cap and shoe molding without additional trial and error.

Installing an Outside Corner Joint

1. Test the angle of outside corners using two pieces of scrap 1x6 stock. Cut a 45-deg. bevel on each piece, and hold them together around the corner. If the joint is not tight, modify the cuts until you achieve a perfect fit.

2. Place masking tape strips on the floor around the corner; then mark along the outside face of the baseboard. Hold stock for each side of the joint in place; use these lines to mark the long point of each miter.

3. For an outside corner, cut and test the fit of the joint before nailing either piece in place. When you are satisfied with the joint, nail the first piece of baseboard to the wall.

4. Apply glue to the surfaces of the miter joint, and place the second piece in position. Make sure that the joint comes together tightly before nailing it to the wall. Use 4d finishing nails or brads.

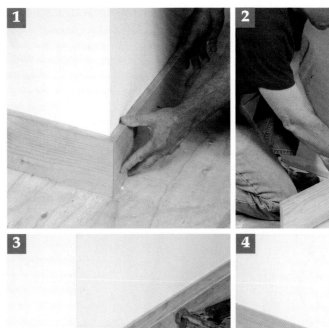

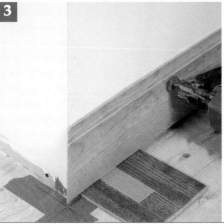

Figuring Corner Angles

While testing an outside corner using test blocks is an efficient method of determining a workable miter angle, there is also a direct approach involving elementary geometry. Fit a sliding bevel gauge around the outside corner, and position it so that the legs are snug to the wall surface. Take the gauge and trace the angle onto a piece of scrap lumber or stiff cardboard. Next, place the point of a compass at the apex of the angle, and scribe an equal distance along each leg of the angle. Reposition the point of the compass at each of these marks and, using the same distance setting, scribe two new intersecting arcs. Draw a line from the apex of the angle through the intersecting point to indicate ½ of the original angle. You can then use an angle gauge to measure the resulting angle, and set your miter saw accordingly.

1 Use a bevel gauge to find the angle; then transfer the angle to a piece of cardboard.

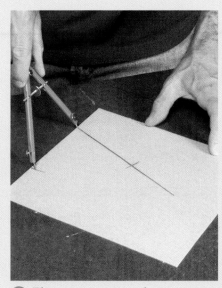

2 Place a compass at the apex of the angle and scribe an arc along each leg.

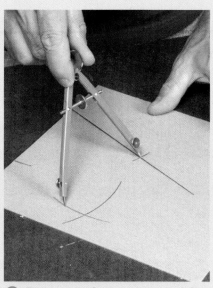

3 Reposition the compass at each of these intersecting marks, and scribe two new intersecting arcs.

4 Draw a line connecting the intersection of the new arcs with the apex of the original angle.

5 Use an angle gauge to measure the resulting angle. Use that setting on the miter saw to cut the joint.

Dealing with Out-of-Level Floors

There are times when a floor is so far from level that you need to adjust the baseboard to accommodate the condition. You might also find that a run of floor has an unusual hump or dip in the surface that is too large to ignore. Small gaps between the floor and baseboard are typically covered by a flexible shoe molding, but extreme cases require that you scribe the molding to fit the contour of the floor.

First cut the baseboard to length, with appropriate joints at either end. Then place shims under the trim piece to support it in position with the top edge level. Set your scribers to a dimension equal to the largest shim dimension, and run the tool along the floor surface to mark a contour line along the face of the baseboard. Use a sharp plane or jig saw to remove stock up to the scribed line. Keep in mind that because you will install shoe molding, a ⅛- to ⅜-inch gap is perfectly acceptable. Remember, if you need to remove stock at the end of a run of baseboard, the adjacent piece will also need to be adjusted so that their top edges will align.

If the floor is dramatically out of level, scribe the baseboard to absorb the discrepancy. Place shims beneath the baseboard to bring it level; then use a scriber to mark the bottom face of the board for the required adjustment.

Three-Piece Base Trim

Using built-up base trim gives you the opportunity to personalize and customize the base treatment. In its simplest incarnation, three-piece trim involves a flat baseboard with added cap and shoe molding. The height of the baseboard and particular profile of the cap molding are yours to decide. You can shape the edge of the base trim to a rounded or chamfered profile, or leave it square.

The heart of a simple three-piece base is ¾-inch flat stock. If you leave the outside edge of the stock square, there is no need to cope the inside corner joints. Simply run the pieces tightly together with butt joints at each inside corner. If you decide to shape a rounded or chamfered edge on the stock, use the router to mill all of the material at one time. Then treat the inside corners as you would any shaped molding, with coped joints.

Cap Molding. Once you have the initial baseboard installed around the room, you can move to the cap molding. Follow the same order of installation that you used for the baseboard, using butt, coped, and mitered joints as necessary. If you need to construct a scarf joint, make sure that the joint does not fall directly over a similar joint in the baseboard.

Shoe Molding. Wait to install the shoe molding until the finished floor surface is installed. As with the cap molding, you can either use another stock profile or fabricate your own molding. Just keep in mind that the molding should be flexible enough to conform to minor irregularities in the floor surface. Use coped joints at the inside corners and miter joints for outside corners. When the shoe molding approaches a casing, plinth block, or wall register, the normal treatment is to cut a partially open 45-degree miter on the end of the molding. Always nail shoe molding to the baseboard, not to the finished floor material.

Nailing Base Trim

Attach baseboard and cap molding to the wall framing. Nail the shoe to the baseboard—never nail the shoe directly to the floor.

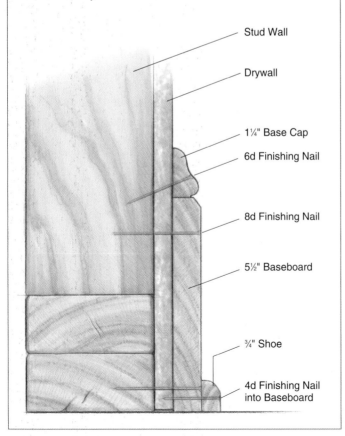

- Stud Wall
- Drywall
- 1¼" Base Cap
- 6d Finishing Nail
- 8d Finishing Nail
- 5½" Baseboard
- ¾" Shoe
- 4d Finishing Nail into Baseboard

---

1. For square stock, use butt joints for inside corner joints. Fit the first piece, and nail it in place. Cut the second piece a few inches long, and test the fit before cutting to length.

2. Once the flat baseboard molding is installed, you can move on to the cap molding. Nail the cap to the wall studs, angling the nails to draw the cap down tightly to the baseboard.

3. At inside corners, cut a coped joint on the second piece of cap molding. Test-fit each piece, and make necessary adjustments with knife, rasp, or sandpaper until you achieve a tight fit.

4. Finished inside corner joint of three-piece base trim. Both cap molding and shoe molding require coped joints at an inside corner.

5. Finished outside corner joint of three-piece base trim. Apply a small amount of glue to the surfaces of miter joints before nailing the molding to the wall.

6. When a shoe molding ends at a plinth block, hold the shoe molding against the block, and place a pencil mark on the end to indicate the exposed portion of the molding.

7. Cut the shoe using an open miter that leaves the layout line in place. Nail the shoe molding to the baseboard using 4d finishing nails. Make sure that you don't nail the molding to the flooring.

8. Detail of three-piece base trim intersection with a Victorian casing and a plinth block. Three-piece base trim complements a number of trimwork styles.

Wall Frames and Wainscoting

Wall frames and wainscoting create a sense of drama and style in a room. They provide focus and a sense of order to an otherwise blank room canvas, and they offer the opportunity to use color and finish options to define the room environment.

Of the two, wall frames are the simpler option to install. They consist of some type of panel molding that is assembled into "frames" and then mounted to the wall. While the basic process is rather simple, the infinite range of frame sizes and shapes allows you the ability to create vastly different looks with the same essential material and technique. Wall frames can be made in either horizontal or vertical configurations, and they can be installed on just the lower portion of a wall, under a chair rail, or above the chair rail as well. If you add in the possible decorative painting and wallpapering options that wall frames provide, you can start to see how rich an alternative this can be.

Wainscoting Designs. Wainscoting is a more labor- and material-intensive approach to wall treatment. It involves applying either boards or frame-and-panel assemblies to the lower part of a wall and capping the installation with an integral chair rail. You can fashion a wainscoting to be compatible with almost any style decor. A simple country- or rustic-style treatment would consist of tongue-and-groove boards with a beaded or V-groove molded profile.

A room in the Arts and Crafts genre would typically feature plain-edge frame stock surrounding flat panels, often in quarter-sawn white oak, cherry, or mahogany, but this style is regularly executed in paint-grade materials as well. For a more layered decor—such as Georgian, Federal, or Greek Revival—panel molding can be added to either a flat-panel or raised-panel design.

The height of a typical wainscoting can vary from 30 to 36 inches, or extend to 60 inches in Arts and Crafts-style rooms. Try to avoid installations that divide the wall height in half, as this can appear awkward.

Wall-frame designs, left, often include the frame, a chair rail, and a subrail.

Decorative paint and paper finishes, above, are an excellent way to complete a frame design.

32" Wall-Frame Treatment
with Horizontal Frame

36" Wall-Frame Treatment
with Horizontal Frame

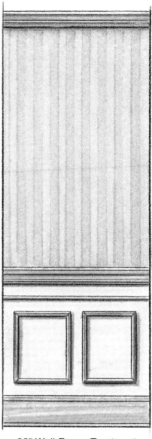

36" Wall-Frame Treatment
with Vertical Frames

60" Wall-Frame Treatment
with Vertical Frames

Wall Frames

Planning a room layout for a wall-frame treatment may be the most complex part of the job. Because the options are so varied, you need to focus on the ultimate look you wish to achieve and work backward toward the specific frame sizes. First decide if you want to apply frames to the entire wall or just the lower portion of the wall. Frames above a chair rail can limit or interfere with the placement of artwork and mirrors, so take these factors into account before you begin. You also have the option of adding a subrail below and parallel with the chair rail to further embellish the lower portion of a wall.

Frame Orientation. Consider the orientation of the wall frames—horizontal or vertical. It is also possible to mix a horizontal orientation below a chair rail with a vertical orientation above the rail. Mixing frames of different dimensions can also provide an intentional and defined sense of balance and proportion in a room. If you want to entertain this option, develop a pattern that can be repeated around the room. In mixing wide and narrow

frames, the outside frames of a pattern should always be the narrow ones, and the grouping should be symmetrical. A short wall can feature one distinct grouping of frames, while on a long wall you can repeat the pattern two or three times.

Wall-Frame Layout. The number of vertical margins, or spaces between frames, is always one more than the number of wall frames on each wall. Position the frames so that the margins are uniform; although small discrepancies should not be noticed at either end of a wall, or where a window or door interrupts the layout.

The margins above and below the frames—for example, the spaces between baseboard and the frame or the chair rail and the frame—can also deviate from the dimension of the vertical spacing; just try to keep the difference minimal. The best way to decide on a layout is to plot each wall surface on a sheet of graph paper, with window and doors drawn to scale. Use tracing paper to experiment with different options. Draw in the baseboard, chair rail, subrail (if appropriate), and cornice molding; then try

Margin spacing, the areas around the frames, should be as consistent as possible, left. Note the angled cut following the path of the staircase.

Create a miniframe, above, to deal with electrical receptacles that fall within a frame.

different frame layouts. If you will be placing frames below a window, the outer edges of the frame should align with the outer edges of the window casing. If you place a frame above a door, the sides of the frame should align with the door casing.

Once you have determined the size of your frames, make a cut list for each of the frame parts. Use a miter saw to cut the panel molding to size with appropriate angles on the ends of each piece. For square frames, make some test cuts on scrap stock to check the accuracy of your saw settings.

TRIM TIP

Although you can sometimes rely on the position of wall framing to provide good nailing for trim members, for wall frames this is often not the case. The arbitrary position of frames can result in a situation where good nailing bases are absent—many frames will fall between wall studs. However, this is one case where you need not be too concerned. Because the frames are extremely lightweight and only decorative in nature, you can use a combination of adhesive and nails to safely hold them to the wall.

Frame Cutting Jig. To simplify assembly of the wall frames, construct a simple jig to help position the parts. Cut a small piece of plywood, about 8 inches on each side, with perfectly square corners—use a try-square to check the cuts. Screw that block to a larger piece of plywood at least 2-foot square. Keep the block back from the panel edge about 1½ inches to create a lip to support the panel molding. Apply glue to the first set of mitered ends, and position them around the gauge block on the jig. Use a brad gun, or a hammer and nail set, to fasten the joints by driving a fastener through the edges of the molding. Join the molding into two L-shaped subassemblies, and then join those to create the frame. Allow the glue to set before fastening the frames to the walls.

As an aid in laying out the frames, rip a block to the width of the top margin (for frames below a chair rail), and use it to scribe a light mark on the wall to indicate the top edge of the frames. Then use a tape measure to mark the locations of the top outside frame corners where they intersect that line. Apply a small bead of panel adhesive to the back side of the first frame, and hold it in place on the guide lines. Use 6d finishing nails to fasten the top edge of the frame to the wall. Check that the sides of the frame are perfectly plumb; then drive nails to fasten them on the remaining three edges. If you notice small spaces between the back of a frame and the wall, apply a small bead of caulk.

Installing Wall Frames

1. Attach a small piece of plywood (with two adjacent factory edges) to a 2 x 2-ft. sheet. Leave a margin of 1½ in.

2. Apply glue to the mitered ends, and fasten them using an air nailer or hammer and brads. Keep your fingers clear.

3. Cut a block the same width as the top margin; place it against the chair rail; and scribe a guideline on the wall.

4. Measure and mark the top corners of each wall frame. Then apply adhesive to the first frame.

5. Using the spacer block from Step 3, align the wall frame with the corner marks, and fasten it in place.

6. With the top edge fastened, plumb the vertical sides of the frame, and attach them using 6d finishing nails.

7. Double-check that the bottom of the frame is level, and then fasten it. Fill all holes, and caulk all around the frame.

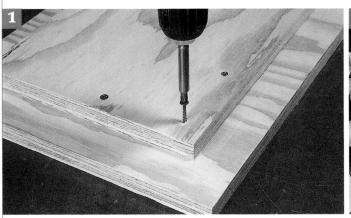

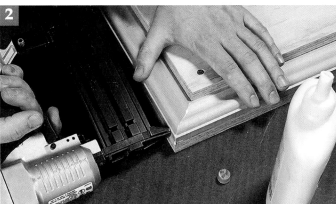

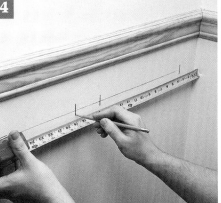

Tongue-and-Groove Bead-Board Wainscoting

One of the simplest and most common types of wainscoting consists of an application of tongue-and-groove boards to the lower portion of a wall. This is a popular treatment in kitchens, bathrooms, and other less-formal rooms in a home.

While the basic installation process is the same regardless of the particular material chosen, you can achieve unique results by selecting different materials for the paneling. A popular choice for this treatment is fir boards with a beaded profile milled into the surface. This material is manufactured in various thicknesses, ranging from ⅜ to ¾ inch, as well as in various width boards, usually between 3 and 5 inches. Beaded-board stock is available as random length milled stock and also in prepackaged kits. In addition, you can also find the same pattern milled into various hardwood species so that you have the flexibility to customize your installation to suit your desired decor. And to further increase your options, you can use other tongue-and-groove stock, such as ¾-inch-thick knotty pine or cedar, following the same basic installation methods.

In all cases, tongue-and-groove wainscoting features an applied base trim and chair-rail cap to complete the installation. The particular configuration of these elements is another area where you can look to personalize your installation. The examples we provide are simply a guide to basic installation techniques; you can easily use these as models for your own designs.

Tongue-and-groove beaded wainscoting is a popular component of casual decorating schemes.

Install Blocking. Because this type of wainscoting requires fastening at frequent intervals along the wall, it is important that you provide blocking for nailing at all necessary points. Of course, you can apply continuous furring strips to the surface of the wall, but this would extend the projection of the wainscoting into the room and could cause problems at those points where it intersects door and window casing. To avoid this problem, determine the height of the top of the wainscoting material; subtract the thickness of the cap; and scribe a level line at that height around the perimeter of the room.

Use a utility knife or drywall saw to cut the drywall along that line, and remove the drywall down to the floor. Then rip panels of ½-inch-thick CD grade plywood to width to replace the drywall.

Nail or screw the plywood panels to the studs and sole-plate of the wall. If you wish to save material, you could install three or four nailing strips instead of full panels, but the time saved and additional backing provided make the full-panel system a good approach.

Cut the Wainscoting. Cut the tongue-and-groove boards to length. For ease of installation, cut the boards about ¼ inch short of the full wainscot height. For a wall with two inside corners, begin the installation at one end. Hold the first board against the corner, with the groove edge toward the corner, and check that it is plumb before nailing it to the backing. If necessary, you can move the board away from the corner at top or bottom to bring it plumb. As long as the gap in the corner will be covered by the adjacent corner board, you do not need to scribe the piece.

Slide the groove of the second board over the tongue of the first strip, and then drive the nails, just above the tongue, angled to drive the boards tightly together. Proceed in this way across the wall until you approach the opposite corner. If you encounter difficulty sliding the tongue and groove joints together, you can fit a small block of the wainscoting stock over the outside tongue and tap it with a hammer.

When you reach the last board, measure the distance at both top and bottom from the V-groove to the face of the adjacent wall. Mark these measurements on the last board; connect the marks; and rip the board to width. Because the wainscoting will continue on the adjacent wall, you can cut the strip about ⅛ inch shy of the mark to make installation easier, or you can cut it for a snug fit and use the corner to wedge it in place.

Installing Bead-Board Wainscoting

1. Mark a level line at the height of the bottom of the wainscoting cap; then use a drywall saw and utility knife to cut the drywall. Remove the drywall from that line to the floor.

2. Install ½-in. CD plywood panels in place of the drywall. Nail or screw the plywood to the wall studs and soleplate.

3. To begin at an inside corner, hold the first board in place, and use a level to check that it is plumb. Make necessary adjustments to nail it to the plywood backer.

Always work so that the tongue of the board is exposed and the grooved edge faces the corner.

4. Use a cutoff piece of wainscoting stock as a block to coax boards together. You can use a hammer to tap on the waste block without damaging the delicate tongue.

5. As you approach an inside corner, take careful measurements between both the top and bottom of the next-to-last board and the corner. Transfer these measurements to the last board, and use a saber saw to cut it to width.

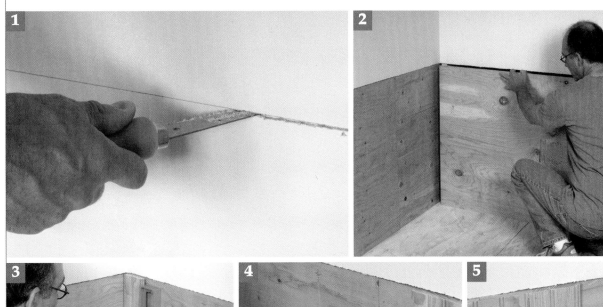

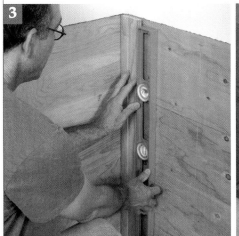

(continued on page 80)

(continued from page 79)

Installing Bead-Board Wainscoting

6. Engage the groove of the last board on a run with the tongue of the previous board, and push it into place. Drive nails through the face of the board in the corner to hold it.

7. Place the first board on the adjacent wall into position, and use a level to check that it is plumb. If it is, nail it in place.

8. If an inside corner is not plumb, hold the first board plumb, and use scribers to mark the face for the adjustment. Use a saber saw or sharp plane to remove the necessary material.

9. For an outside corner joint, create a tight butt joint by first ripping the groove off of the first board. Use sandpaper or a sharp plane to remove saw marks.

10. The second half of an outside corner requires that you remove the groove plus an amount equal to the thickness of the stock to create an equal reveal on each side of the corner.

11. Use a level to check that the first board at an outside corner is plumb. Allow the outer edge of the board to protrude just beyond the backer so you can fashion a tight corner joint.

12. Apply a small bead of glue to the outside corner joint; then nail the two boards together.

13. Use a sharp plane to shape a bevel on the outside corner of wainscoting panel stock.

Typical Corner Construction

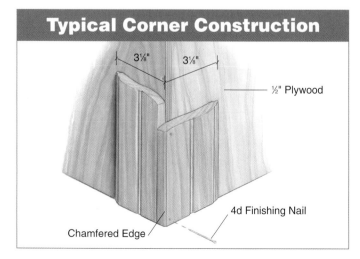

3⅛"   3⅛"

½" Plywood

4d Finishing Nail

Chamfered Edge

Adjoining Wall. Hold the first strip on the next wall in position, and check that its leading edge is plumb. If necessary, adjust the strip so that it is plumb; then measure the resulting gap and set a scriber to that dimension. Continue holding the strip in position as you run the scriber along the joint to mark the necessary adjustment. Remember to keep both wings of the scriber parallel with the floor as you move it down the joint. Use a sharp block plane to remove the required stock; then test the fit of the board. Once you are satisfied with the joint, nail the strip in place.

Outside Corners. If your room includes an outside corner joint, you should begin the installation there so that you can ensure a neat and balanced joint at this

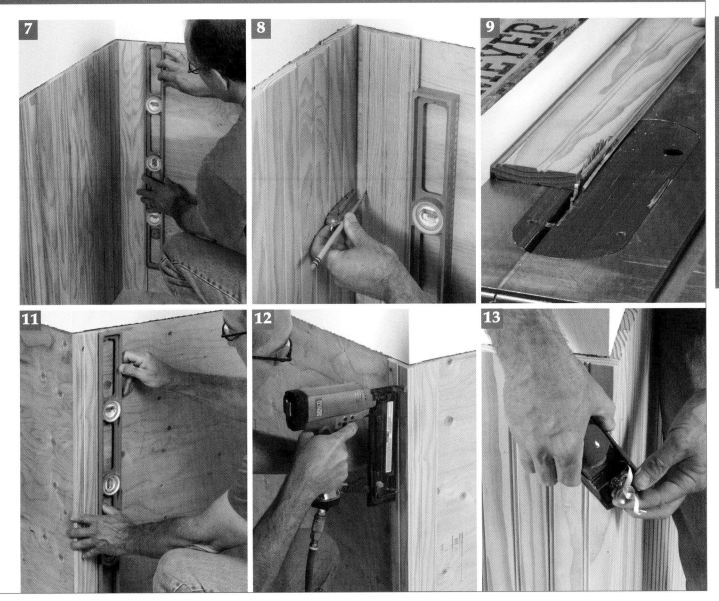

more visible point. Rip the groove off of one board to form one half of the corner joint. Next, rip the width of the groove plus the thickness of the wainscoting stock off the adjacent corner board. This detail ensures that when you assemble the two pieces at the corner you will have a symmetrical reveal on each face. (See the sequence of steps 9 through 13, above, and "Typical Corner Construction," opposite.)

Install the narrower board on the corner first; once more, check that it is plumb before nailing it in place. Allow the edge of the board to extend just beyond the corner so that you can be sure of achieving a tight joint. Hold the wider corner board in place. If necessary, adjust the board so that it is plumb, and plane off the required stock so that it does not project beyond the corner. Apply

glue to the joint and install the second corner board using nails. You can later plane a new bevel on the outside edge of the corner to provide a finished appearance to the joint.

Baseboard and Chair Rail. Apply baseboard and chair-rail molding to the wall. Depending on the configuration of your window and door trim, these elements might project beyond the face of the casing. In that situation, you will need to fashion a neat return or end treatment at each opening. Because the range of possible situations is vast, examine our example for a suggested approach; then feel free to devise an appropriate solution for your own installation. (See "Adding Baseboard and Chair Rail," page 82.)

1. Nail baseboard to the wainscoting panel stock. Remember to use appropriate spacers for carpeting, hardwood, or tile flooring.

2. Cut miters for the outside corners of apron molding. Test-fit the joints to check for proper fit; then apply a bead of glue; and nail the molding in place.

3. It's common for drywall surfaces to flare out at the corners. Cut the stock to length with appropriate end joints; then use a scriber to mark the required adjustment on the face of the cap.

4. Nail the chair-rail cap to the top edge of wainscoting panels and apron molding; then pin the miter joint together using a 4d finishing nail or brad.

5. Finished outside corner detail of wainscoting chair rail.

6. Finished inside corner detail of wainscoting chair rail. Note butt joint for square-edge cap stock.

7. Mark the end of the apron molding to indicate the depth of the casing. Then cut an open 45-deg. miter that meets the face of the casing. Nail the apron to the wainscot paneling.

8. Cut a notch in the chair-rail cap stock to fit tightly to the casing. Ease the edges of the cap, or shape a rounded end; then nail it to the top edges of apron and wainscot paneling.

Dealing with Electrical Boxes

As you proceed across the wall, it is inevitable that you will encounter electrical outlets. Make sure that the electrical circuits are turned off; then remove the cover plates and outlets. When you approach an outlet box, take careful measurements from the edge of the last strip before the box to determine its position. Mark the location of your cutout on the board and, if necessary, drill clearance holes in each corner so that you can insert a saber saw blade.

Use the saw to make the required cutout. For ease of installation, allow about 1/16 inch extra space around the box on all sides. Test the fit of the board, and make any necessary adjustments. If the electrical box straddles two boards, mark and cut the second part of the cutout, and mount the second board. Remember to provide clearance for the outlet mounting screws. Depending on the thickness of your wainscoting and local electrical codes, you might need to install extension sleeves to the electrical boxes before reinstalling the outlets.

1 Measure the distance between an outlet box and the nearest full board. Transfer the measurements to a piece of wainscoting stock. Allow an additional 1/8 in. for adjustments.

2 Transfer the height of the bottom and top of an electrical box directly to the wainscoting stock. Use a saber saw to make the necessary cutout. Make sure that you leave clearance for the outlet mounting screws.

3 If required, install an extension to the existing electrical box. Slide it into position, and make the necessary electrical connections.

Panel Dimensions. Experiment with the placement of frame stiles to achieve a pleasing division of space across the wall. The width of your panels does not need to be identical on each wall; however, the general proportions of the panels should be close. Once you have determined the layout for the room, plan the size of the plywood panels so that seams will be covered by the stiles.

If you are working in a newly constructed room, apply ½-inch-thick plywood to the wall studs up to the height of the top rail to serve as both the panel faces and frame backer; then apply drywall to the remaining sections of the wall. If you are renovating an existing room, remove the drywall up to the rail height, and install the plywood in its place.

Attach the panels using finishing nails, about 8 inches on center along the studs and soleplate. Set the nailheads slightly below the panel surface. Any fasteners that remain visible after applying the frame parts can easily be filled prior to finishing. If you wish to reduce the number of nails, you can apply a bead of panel adhesive to each stud before placing the panel. Using adhesive, you can fasten the panels only at the top, bottom, and center. Remember to cut the panel stock so that the seams between adjacent panels fall behind a frame stile.

Electrical Boxes. Once again, you will need to make provisions for electrical outlets as you apply the plywood backer. Carefully measure the locations of outlet boxes and transfer them to the first panel. Use a drill to bore clearance holes for the saw blade; then use a saber saw to make the cutouts. Allow an ⅛-inch margin around the box for adjustment.

Depending on your situation, you may need to install box extensions to comply with local building and electrical codes. In some cases you may have to move the boxes so that they are flush with the new finished wall surface. If possible, it is best to lay out the stiles so that they do not fall over an outlet, but sometimes this cannot be avoided. In those cases, you will definitely need to move the box so that it comes flush with the face of the frame. For challenging electrical adaptations, it is always best to call an electrician.

Use a similar approach for heating and air conditioning registers. You can generally treat them in the same way you would when running simple baseboard. Duct extensions are available for almost any type of duct, so you can adapt your installation for registers that fall either in the panel or base trim.

Clamp a stile to the worktable before using the plate joiner to cut slots in the end-grain. End-grain cuts are particularly liable to kick back, and this technique keeps hands far from the spinning blade.

Installing Flat-Panel Wainscoting

1. If you must deal with electrical receptacles, mark the outline of the boxes on the plywood panels.

2. Allow ⅛ in. on each side for ease of installation and adjustment. Use a saber saw to make the cutout for the boxes. Attach the panels to studs.

3. Clamp a bottom and top rail together to mark the locations of the frame stiles. Place a mark to indicate the center of each stile to use when cutting slots for joining plates.

4. Use the plate joiner to cut slots in the top and bottom rails. Firmly press both the joiner and rail stock to the table top to accurately register the slots.

5. Cut blocks to support the bottom rails at the proper height. Use a 4-ft. level to check for level. If necessary, place shims below one or more of the blocks to adjust the position of the rail.

6. Nail the bottom rail to the plywood panel. Place two nails every 16 in. along the length of the rail.

7. Spread glue on a joining plate as well as in the matching slots. Place the plate into the slot in the rail before installing the first stile.

8. Use a short level to check that the first stile is plumb before nailing it. The adjacent corner stile will cover the inside edge, so a small gap at top or bottom won't be visible.

9. Apply glue to joining plates and matching slots before installing the top rail to the ends of stiles.

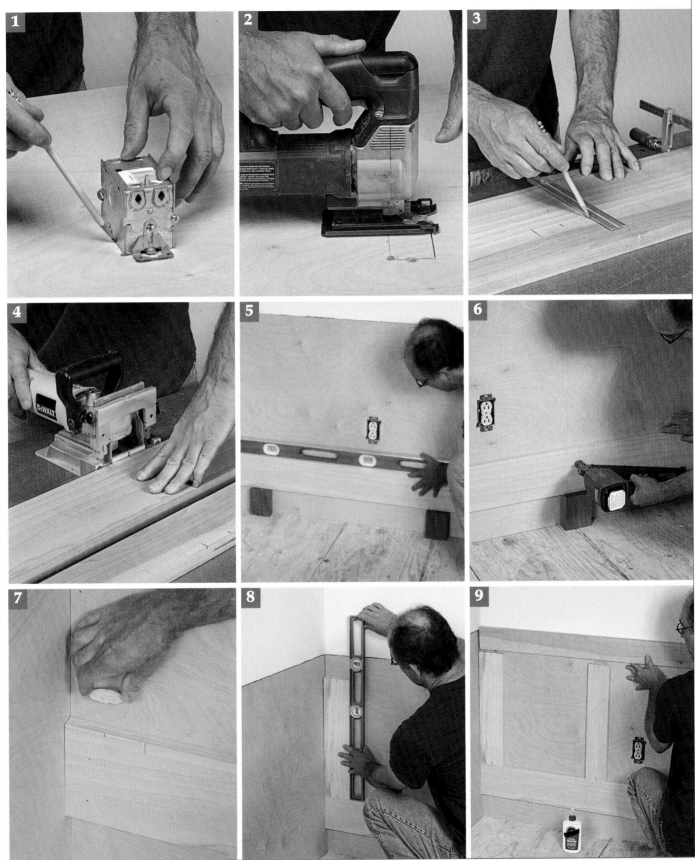

(continued on page 88)

(continued from page 87)

Installing Flat-Panel Wainscoting

10. If the joints between the top rail and stiles are reluctant to close, you can use a clamp to pull the rail into position before nailing it to the plywood backer.

11. To maintain uniform stile exposure on each side of a corner, rip the first stile ¾ in. narrower than normal. Place the second stile in position, and nail the corner joint together.

12. Rip narrow strips to act as backers to support the bottom edge of base trim. Nail the strips to the plywood panel at floor level.

13. Place baseboard in position, and nail it to both the bottom rail and backer strip. After all baseboards are installed, run the cap molding around the room.

14. Cut cove apron molding to size with appropriate end joints; then nail it to the top rail. Keep the molding flush with the top edge of the rail. Add the cap.

15. To add molding to wainscoting panels, first cut the molding to length with 45-deg. miters at each end. Test fit all four pieces; when satisfied, nail them to the plywood panel.

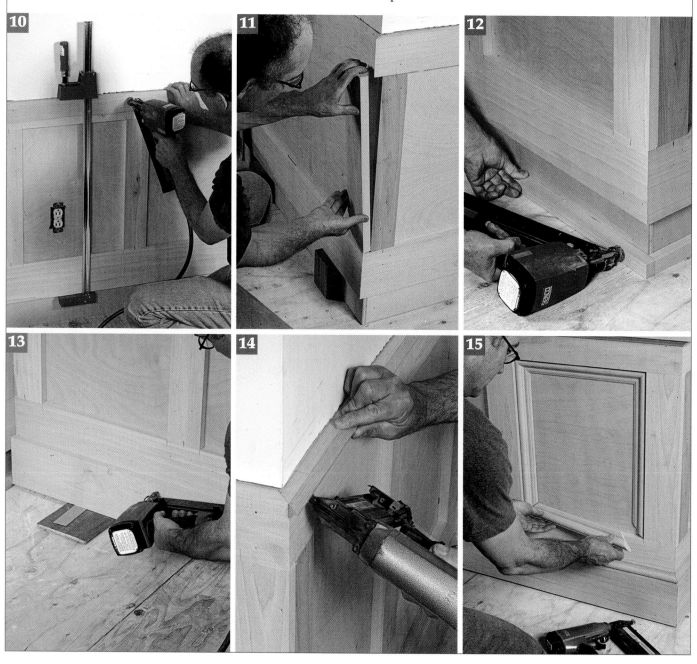

Cut the Rails. Determine the length of the rails for your first wall and crosscut the stock to length. If you need to splice two pieces together to span the wall, use a scarf joint where the sections come together. Temporarily clamp the top and bottom rails together, with their face sides up, and mark the position of the frame stiles. If you wish to avoid pencil marks on parts that will receive a stained or clear finish, apply some masking tape to the faces, and place your marks on the tape. Also place a light mark to indicate the center of each stile. Use these marks to cut joining plate slots in the rail edges for the stile joints. Repeat the process for the rails for each wall section.

If your room includes one or more outside corners, you should cut miter joints on the rails to avoid exposing end grain. These joints can be made using the same techniques you would employ for baseboard stock.

Cut the Stiles. Next, cut stock to size for the stiles. As a general rule, the exposed width of all stiles should be the same. This means that at inside corners, the first stile to be installed will need to be ¾ inch wider than a normal stile. At an outside corner, the first stile installed will need to be ¾ inch narrower than a normal stile. The length of all stiles should be identical, so you can speed the task by putting a stop on the miter saw stand to eliminate the need to measure each piece. Mark a line to indicate the center of each stile, at both top and bottom, and use the plate joiner to cut the slots.

Install Bottom Rail. Cut small blocks from scrap stock to support the bottom rail at the predetermined height. Place the first rail on top of the blocks, and check using a 4-foot level. If necessary, place shims under one or more of the block to level the rail. (See steps 5 and 6, pages 86–87.)

Then begin at one corner and install the first stile. Spread a bit of glue in the mating plate slots and on the joining plate and assemble the stile to the bottom rail. Use a level to check that the stile is plumb, and apply pressure to the rail/stile joint to keep it closed while you drive nails to lock the stile in place. Repeat the procedure for each stile. When you have installed all the stiles on one wall, apply glue to the slots in the top rail and stiles, install joining plates to the slots in the stiles, and position the rail. Once again, apply downward pressure to close the joints while you nail the rail to the backer panel. If the rail is bowed and you have trouble closing a joint, you can use a clamp to pull the parts together.

Proceed around the room, installing the panel frames on one wall at a time. To fashion an outside corner joint, you can miter the rails and stiles together, but it is difficult to achieve good results in the field. A perfectly respectable alternative is to lap the second side over the end of the first one applied. Remember to apply a bead of glue to the joint; then use 4d finishing nails to pin the joint together.

Consider constructing the panels in a workshop and then moving them to the site for installation. If you have space for this, you can use clamps to pull all of the connections tight, and you can attach the plywood backer to the frame by screwing through the backside, eliminating the need to fill nailholes. Add finish molding when the panels are in place. Be sure to measure the room and your work carefully.

Base Trim. Install strips of continuous blocking to the bottom edge of the plywood backer to support the base trim. Then install base trim using the same techniques you would use if there were no wainscoting.

Cove Apron Molding. Install the apron molding flush with the top edge of the top rail; miter outside corner joints; and cope inside corner joints. Rip stock to width for the wainscoting cap. The cap should be wide enough to cover the top rail and apron molding plus an overhang of about ¾ inch. If you wish to put a profiled edge on the stock, use the router table to cut the profile before you rip it from a wider board. For inside corners on the wainscoting cap, you can use either a coped, butt, or inside miter joint, depending on the cap profile.

Apply a bead of glue to the top rail, and place the cap in position. Nail the cap to the top edge of the rail and apron molding. Continue around the room, installing one piece at a time, fitting the joints carefully.

Complete the Panels. If you want to further embellish your wainscoting, you can install molding around the perimeter of each panel. The specific molding that you select should be in keeping with the overall design scheme for your room. For a simple treatment, a cove, beaded, or chamfered molding might be appropriate, while a more formal design might call for an elaborate panel molding.

Installing these moldings is not difficult, but it is labor intensive. Each piece must be either measured or scribed individually, and you must take the time to make accurate miter cuts or the results will reflect shoddy workmanship. If you have installed the panel frames accurately, the corners of each panel should be a 90-degree angle, and your miter cuts can all be 45 degrees. Measure, cut, and, install the molding pieces for one panel at a time to reduce confusion. It is always best when cutting to err slightly on the long side and have to trim a piece to fit, rather than cut a part too short. Always test the fit of all four pieces for each panel before nailing any one of them in place. When you are satisfied with the fit, use brads or 4d finishing nails to fasten the molding to the plywood backer.

ceiling moldings

Cornices & Crown Molding

While it is not necessary that a cornice be part of a comprehensive trim upgrade in a particular room, whatever design you plan should be in keeping with the prevailing spirit of a room. For example, an elaborate Victorian-style treatment would be inappropriate in an Arts and Crafts-style dining room. In addition, the size of the cornice should be in proportion to the ceiling height in the room. Ceilings that are 8 feet high or less cannot support an extremely wide molding, so try to keep the trim from extending more than 4 inches from the ceiling. On the other hand, rooms with ceilings over 9 feet high need wider and more substantial moldings. In these cases, aim for a cornice that drops at least 5 inches from the ceiling surface.

Cornice Materials

Like other millwork items, cornice trim is available in a variety of materials—some for paint-grade work and some that can receive a clear or stained finish. For trim that is to be painted, the most common options are clear or finger-jointed pine and poplar. However, a wide range of profiles are also manufactured in MDF, resin, and polystyrene foam. Each of these materials has its advantages and limitations, but it is certainly worth considering these materials.

MDF Cornices. MDF moldings are manufactured from a mixture of finely ground wood fibers and glue and are shaped under heat and pressure to various profiles. The resulting product is stiff and flat, without defects, and it machines very easily. This is an excellent choice for paint-grade work because it features a very smooth surface with no discernable grain. It can be drilled, nailed, and glued much like wood, and it accepts both latex and oil–based paints. If you will be nailing by hand, you should plan on drilling pilot holes for finishing nails, but pneumatic nail guns will easily drive fasteners through it.

Polyurethane Cornices. Resin moldings are available in an increasing number of profiles and sizes, and in rigid and flexible formulations. It is especially valuable for situations where you need to trim a curved wall surface—either concave or convex. Some manufacturers will provide flexible resin moldings to match stock profiles that they offer in wood trim, so you can mix materials for different parts of a job.

Polystyrene Cornices. Plastic, or polystyrene, molding is a choice that appeals to many do-it-yourselfers. This material is manufactured in a variety of simple and intricate profiles that can mimic vintage plaster moldings at a fraction of the cost of the real thing—if you could even find the real thing. In addition, plastic moldings are extremely lightweight, and you can install them easily and quickly without the necessity of cutting fancy joints. Plastic molding is typically available with matching corner and connecting trim blocks that will allow you to limit your cutting to square butt joints. And for those situations where you do not want to use those blocks, gaps in both inside and outside miter joints can easily be filled with caulk or joint compound.

Wood Cornices. Of course, for stained or clear-finished trim, your most widely available choices are clear pine or red oak moldings. These species are usually stocked at lumberyards and home centers. And specialty millwork houses offer a much wider selection of profiles that can be produced in any species that you choose. If you are thinking about a clear or stained finish for your cornice trim, however, keep in mind that the level of execution needs to be extremely high, and the time involved to do the job will be proportionate to those demands. Caulk is not available for clear-finished trim. As a result, the fit of each coped and mitered joint must be tight all along the profile, and gaps between a molding and the wall or ceiling must often be scribed rather than filled. You can reasonably expect that the time required will be two or three times that for a paint-grade job.

Decorative Corner Blocks

If the prospect of cutting all those coped and mitered joints is just too overwhelming, there are fittings available that eliminate the need for those demanding joints. Much like plinth and corner blocks for baseboard, there are also decorative blocks that can be used for cornice trim. These elements are available in wood, resin, and polystyrene, and it is not even necessary that you use the same material for the blocks as for the rest of the trim members—as long as everything will be painted. Blocks are available for inside and outside corners, and also as connectors to be used in place of scarf joints.

Eliminate cutting by using decorative corner blocks for cornice applications. Those shown here are made of resin.

Installing Crown Molding

The most popular cornice treatment involves installing a one-piece crown molding. These profiles are designed to sit at an angle to both the wall and ceiling, and that angle is known as the spring angle. Most crown molding falls into one of two *spring angle* categories—45/45-degree moldings and 52/38-degree moldings. These descriptions correspond to the angles the molding forms with the ceiling and wall. It is important that you determine the spring angle for your molding, as it affects not only how you mount the molding between wall and ceiling, but how you position it in the miter box to cut the joints.

Cutting with a Miter Saw. If you will be using a simple miter saw to cut crown molding stock, the basic technique involves holding the molding upside down against the saw or miter box fence. The concept to keep in mind is that the saw fence is acting as the wall and the saw table is acting as the ceiling, and when making a cut you

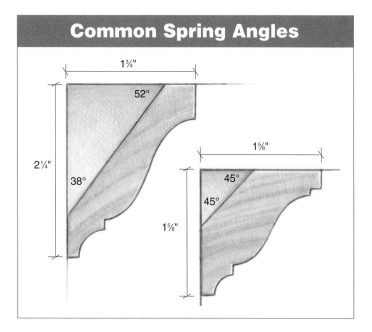

Common Spring Angles

Basic Miter Saw Cuts

Inside corner, left side cope.
Place the molding bottom up on the saw's table. (Note that the cove detail is at the top.) Position the molding so that the excess will fall to the left.

Inside corner, right side cope.
With the molding bottom up, reposition the miter gauge to the left 45-deg. mark. The excess falls to the right.

Outside corner, left side miter.
With the gauge set on the left and the molding bottom up, cut so that the excess falls on the left.

Outside corner, right side miter.
Move the gauge to the right. Turn the bottom of the molding up, and cut so that the excess falls on the right.

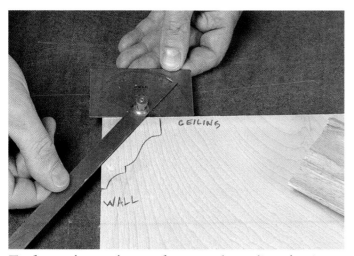

To determine spring angles, trace the outline of a piece of crown molding on a square panel corner. Make sure that the edges of the molding sit flush to the panel edges. Then use an angle gauge to measure the spring angle.

need to hold the molding at the appropriate spring angle between the two registration surfaces. In order to cut an accurate miter angle, you must take care that the spring angle is maintained in every case, with the edges of the molding sitting squarely against both the fence and table, before making the cut. Until you become comfortable with the orientation of the molding in the saw, it is easy to get confused. To avoid mistakes in cutting, it is a good idea to take some extra molding stock and cut test joints on four pieces—a left and right outside miter for outside corner joints, and a left and right inside miter, which will be used to cope inside corner joints. Then you can refer to the proper sample piece to ensure that your saw and molding setup are correct.

Cutting Using a Compound Miter Saw. When using a compound miter saw, the technique is different because you can make the cuts with the stock held flat on the saw table. First, determine the spring angle of your particular

Compound Miter Saw Cuts

Inside corner, left side cope. Tilt the saw to the correct angle, and set the miter gauge to the right. Place the molding so that the top faces the fence and the excess falls to the right.

Inside corner, right side cope. With the saw tilted, set the miter gauge to the left. Place the molding so that the bottom faces the fence and the excess falls to the right.

Outside corner, left side miter. With the saw tilted, set the miter gauge to the left. Place the molding so that the bottom faces the fence and the excess falls to the left.

Outside corner, right side miter. With the saw tilted, set the miter gauge to the right. Place the molding so that the top faces the fence and the excess falls to the left.

crown molding. To cut a 90-degree corner on 45-degree molding, tilt the saw to a 30-degree bevel angle and set the miter angle to either 35.3 degrees left or 35.3 degrees right. To cut a 90-degree corner on 52/38-degree molding, tilt the saw to a bevel angle of 33.9 degrees and set the miter angle to either 31.6 degrees left or 31.6-degrees right.

Saw settings for joints that occur at angles other than 90 degrees can be found in the chart that usually comes with the saw. You can use an adjustable angle gauge to determine the angle of any corner. Just keep in mind that the reading is not guaranteed to be accurate because of flared corners or dips in the wall surface. Use the angle reading as a starting point for cutting the joint and always test the angle using scrap stock before cutting expensive moldings. Orient the molding on the saw table according to the photos on page 93 to make the appropriate cuts for miter and cope joints. Once again, it is a good idea to make sample cuts on some short pieces of crown mold-

ing. Label these for each type of joint you will be cutting, and use them to test your setup when readjusting the compound miter saw.

Evaluate the Room. Before starting your installation, it is important that you examine both the walls and ceiling for any potential problems that could affect the molding. The most common difficulty that you will find is a dip in the ceiling. Hold a long, straight 2x4 or 1x4 against the ceiling, near the wall, to test for straightness. If the surfaces are without serious defect, you can install the molding without making any major adjustments, but if bumps or dips are present, you have three options to consider.

Fixing Problems. If the irregularities are minor, you can usually bend the molding to conform to the shape of the ceiling. And if small gaps exist, you can caulk them after priming the trim. Keep in mind, though, that bending the crown too severely may result in a visible distortion of the

Cutting Crown Molding Using a Hand Miter Saw

When using a hand or power miter saw, it is critical to hold a crown molding at the proper spring angle for accurate miter cuts. One way to ensure that the molding sits at the right angle is to create a jig to support the stock. First, fashion an auxiliary table and fence for the saw by screwing together two pieces of 1-by pine

stock. Clamp this assembly to the saw, and use a small cut-off piece of the appropriate crown molding, held at the appropriate angle, as a guide to mark lines on the saw table. Place wooden strips in position, on the outer side of those lines, and screw them to the table. Use the jig to guide your cuts.

 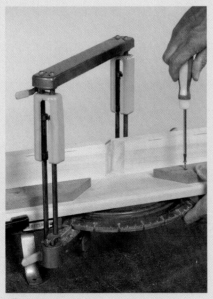 

1 Use a short piece of crown molding as a guide to mark lines on the miter saw table for placement of support strips.

2 Screw support strips to the auxiliary miter saw table to hold crown molding at the proper spring angle.

3 Place a length of crown molding in the miter saw with its top edge resting on the saw table against the support strip.

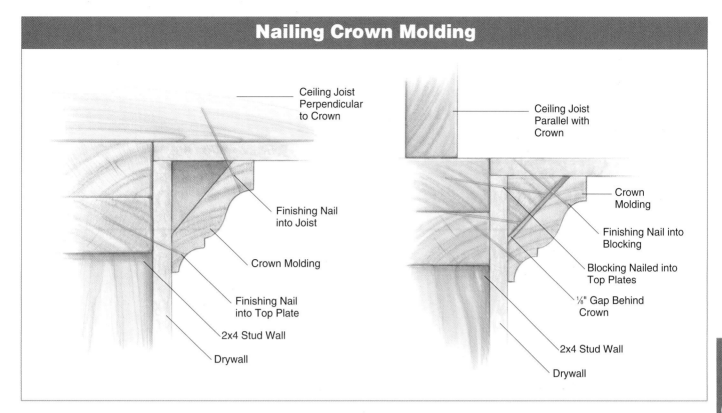

Ceiling Joist Perpendicular to Crown

Finishing Nail into Joist

Crown Molding

Finishing Nail into Top Plate

2x4 Stud Wall

Drywall

Ceiling Joist Parallel with Crown

Crown Molding

Finishing Nail into Blocking

Blocking Nailed into Top Plates

⅛" Gap Behind Crown

2x4 Stud Wall

Drywall

molding, and this might be more distracting than other options. Too much stress on a molding can also cause problems at the corner joints because the spring angle can be difficult to maintain.

A second approach is to hold a length of molding in place at the most extreme defect, and mark the bottom edge on the adjacent wall surface. Use that mark as a reference in establishing a level line around the room, and set the crown to that line. This will result in gaps at certain points between the crown and ceiling, but if they are not too large, you can fill them with caulk or joint compound.

Another option, and the most difficult, is to scribe the crown to fit around any dips or bumps in the walls or ceiling. If your crown molding is to be stained or will receive a clear finish, this is the best approach. First, cut the molding to length with appropriate joints at either end; then have a helper assist you in holding the molding in place against the wall and ceiling. Mark the areas that need to be adjusted, and use a sharp block plane to remove the necessary stock. Proceed slowly, testing the fit of the molding frequently so that you do not remove too much material.

Installing Blocking. Because crown molding spans the joint between wall and ceiling, it must be fastened to both surfaces to maintain its position. While you can rely on having studs and a top plate to accept nails on the wall side of the molding, you can only count on ceiling joists running perpendicular to half of the walls in a room. On the remaining walls, where the joists run parallel with the wall surface, there is often no framing member where you require one for nailing at the ceiling. You can easily solve this problem by installing backer blocks around the room to accept nails wherever necessary. Cut 2-by stock to form blocks, at the appropriate spring angle, that you can nail to the wall studs and top plate. Cut the blocks to allow a space of about ⅛ inch between the molding and block so that you have some room to adjust the molding during installation.

Plan the Layout. As with base trim, it is important to plan the order of installation of crown molding. The primary difference with ceiling trim is that there are generally no doorways or other room openings to consider. For wooden crown molding, the convention of using coped joints at inside corners and miter joints at outside corners is one to take seriously. Inside miter joints are extremely likely to open over time, if not directly upon installation. In a basic installation—a rectangular room with four walls—the first piece of crown can be installed with two square ends that butt tightly to the wall surfaces. Thereafter, you should proceed around the room with the next two pieces having one coped end and one square end. The final piece of molding will require two coped ends. Because it is difficult, even for a professional carpenter, to carefully fit a piece of molding with coped joints on both ends, you can fit each corner on separate pieces and then cut a scarf joint to join the two pieces into one continuous length.

Installing Crown Molding

1 Once you've established your guideline location, snap a chalk line for the molding.

4 Install the full-length square-cut cornice, fitting it into the corner. Don't nail within 3 or 4 ft. of the corner yet.

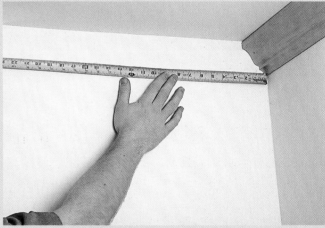

5 Measure out from the corner (plus an extra couple of inches) to find the rough length of the coped molding.

8 Rotate the saw as needed to maneuver the thin blade along the profile of the miter.

9 Use an oval-shaped file (or a round file in tight spots) to clean up curved sections of the profile.

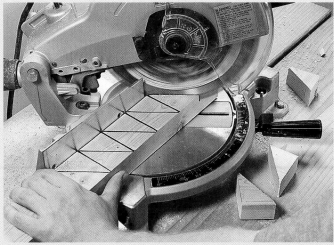

2 Match the angle of the molding installation to the angle of the nailers, and cut them on your power miter saw.

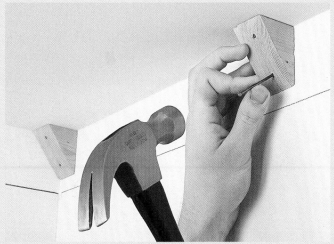

3 Nail or screw the support blocks to wall studs and the wall top plate every 16 in.

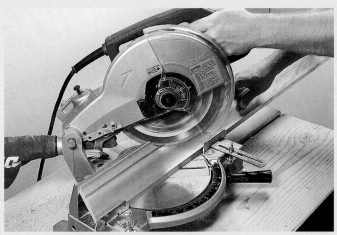

6 Cut the coping miter on another board, and transfer the dimension from Step 5, measuring from the miter tip.

7 Use a coping saw to start the profile cut. Angle the saw to back-cut the coped piece

10 Use a flat rasp as needed to clean up the upper section of the coped cut or to increase the back-cut angle.

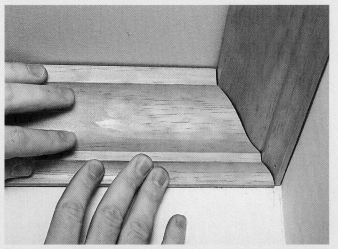

11 Test-fit the coped piece in place, supporting the other end to be sure the board is level. *(continued on page 98)*

(continued from page 97)

Installing Crown Molding

12 Double-check your measurements, and trim off any extra wood from the rough measurement.

13 Adjust and fit the pieces; support the coped piece in place; and drill near the coped end to avoid splitting.

Inside Corners

It can be difficult to achieve tight inside corner joints even when all conditions are perfect. And because those conditions rarely exist, expect that some fussing and refitting will be necessary, especially when you first begin a job. Corners that are not perfectly square, and walls and ceilings that are not absolutely flat can modify the spring angle and change the profile of the required cope. To make your life easier, it's worth doing all you can to allow some flexibility in the joint. One technique you can employ is to refrain from nailing within 2 feet of the corner on the first piece of molding that you install on an inside corner joint. Then when you test the fit of the coped joint, the first piece is not secured fast to the wall, and you have the ability to adjust the position of that piece to better correspond to the coped profile.

For pieces that require a coped joint, cut the stock a few inches longer than the wall; then fashion and test the fit of the coped end before laying out the finished length. This provides you with some latitude to get the coped joint right without worrying about the overall length of the section of molding.

If the molding must fit between two walls, you will have to hold the opposite end away from the wall to test the fit. Of course, molding that ends at an outside corner should be held in place to be carefully marked for exact length.

Outside Corners. In rooms that include an outside corner joint, you can often avoid the necessity of having to cut coped joints on both ends of a length of molding. In this case, you can save the outside corner to be the last joint that you fit. And because it is an open-ended joint, you can fit the coped corner first and then hold the molding in place to mark the final length of the outside miter.

When cutting molding that fits between two walls, add at least 1/16 inch to the measurement before cutting the stock to length. The additional length will ensure a tight joint at the ends of the molding, but it will require you to "spring" the molding into position. As a general rule, follow this technique when cutting pieces that fit between two surfaces, as the additional tension can help close joints that are otherwise a bit open, or keep well-fitting joints from opening in the future.

Crown molding is often used as a cornice treatment, but it can also add a distinctive look to cabinetry.

14 Apply wood glue to sections of the coped end that will make contact with the square-end piece.

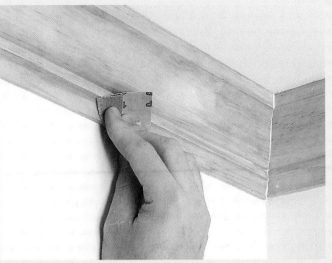

15 To finish, drive and set finishing nails to secure the corner pieces, and sand or caulk the joint as needed.

Installing Outside Corners

1. Cut and fit the coped joint first; then hold the section in place and mark for cutting.

2. Trim the molding, and cut a miter joint on the end. Do the same for the adjoining piece.

3. Install the pieces by applying a bead of carpenter's glue to the joint and securing using finishing nails.

4. Smooth the joint so that the molding appears to be a continuous piece. Use a nail set to knock down the edge.

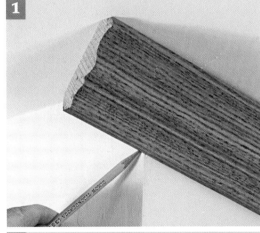

Installing Built-up or Compound Cornice Trim

For rooms with high ceilings, or for any situation where you want a more elaborate ceiling molding, consider a built-up or layered approach to the cornice. Even a room with an 8-foot ceiling can accept this type of treatment, providing the cornice is in proper proportion to the scale of the room. The cornice can be as simple as pairing a frieze of inverted baseboard or 1-by pine with a crown molding, or complex, such as combining several different profiles that complement each other. A built-up cornice does not need to include an angled crown molding. It can include two or more types of flat molding stock applied to just the wall or both wall and ceiling.

Profile Choices. Common elements that are used in built-up cornices include dentil, egg and dart, cove, bead, bed, and crown molding, although your actual choices are certainly not limited to those options. The best way to proceed in developing a design is to study

Installing a Built-Up Cornice

1 Hold the backer in place against the ceiling to drill pilot holes for screws. Drill through backer and into the ceiling to mark the location of spiral anchors where necessary.

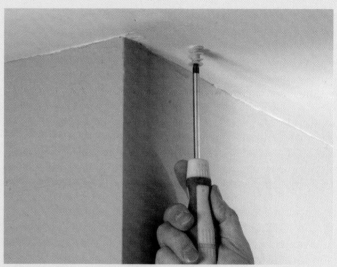

2 Install spiral anchors wherever you cannot locate a ceiling joist for blocking attachment.

6 Cut flat miters for outside corners of the soffit trim, and nail the soffit to the backer. Fashion coped joints for inside corners. Cut miter joints for outside corners, and nail the crown to both the soffit and frieze.

7 Nail the fascia to the soffit and backer boards. Position the fascia so that it projects ¼ in. below the soffit.

available molding profiles and draw full-scale cross sections of different combinations so that you can better envision them. You can use the samples in the drawings on pages 102–103 as a guide in designing your cornice. When you arrive at a prospective design, purchase short sections of each molding; assemble a sample block of the cornice that is 1 or 2 feet long—you can use nails or even hot glue to hold the parts together—and hold it up to the ceiling. This will allow you to best judge whether the proportions and particular moldings are correct. While

this may seem excessively cautious, remember that the investment in both materials and time for a cornice of this type is considerable. The worst case scenario has you completing the job only to realize that the trim seems totally out of place in the room. An additional bonus to making the sample cornice is that you actually go through the assembly process, seeing how the various components to together. This can be very helpful in planning the sequence of steps you will go through when installing the molding on the wall.

3 Screw through the blocking to fasten it to the ceiling. Drive the screws into ceiling joists or spiral anchors to form a base for cornice trim.

4 Mark a level line to indicate the bottom edge of the frieze. Use screws to fasten the frieze to wall studs or top plate.

5 Cut an open miter to prepare for cutting the coped profile at an inside corner. Test the fit, and make necessary adjustments.

8 Install bed molding between the fascia and ceiling. If necessary, you can caulk any gaps between the molding and ceiling or wall surfaces.

9 Completed built-up cornice. The goal is to make the multiple components look like one piece of molding.

Typical Built-Up Cornice Profiles

3¼" Colonial Base

1x2

1¾" Bed Molding

¾" x 2" Soffit

¾" x 2¾" Blocking

3¼" Crown

1x4

2⁷⁄₁₆" Chair Rail

¾" Cove

1x4

Shoe Molding

Blocking and Backing. In some cases, you will need to provide blocking to support a built-up cornice, and in other situations none will be required. In more elaborate designs, continuous backing is often the best choice because it is good practice to stagger scarf joints, and the backer allows you to locate these joints at any convenient spot.

In a built-up cornice, it is always best to establish a level line to define the bottom edge of the trim element against the wall. Then if you encounter deviations in the height of the ceiling from that line, you can take up the difference between two or more molding elements and make the discrepancy less visible. As a general rule, those viewing a finished cornice installation tend not to notice small variations in the reveals between profiles from one part of a room to another—things that can seem quite problematic, and obvious, to the installer.

Most built-up cornices involve some type of frieze that is mounted to the wall and serves as the base for other profiles. The frieze serves as a decorative element as well as blocking to accept the nails to hold them in place. It can be made from 1x4 stock, either with or without a molded edge, or a piece of inverted baseboard molding. Once you have established your level line, it is a simple matter to install the frieze to the wall. If you are using stock without a molded edge, inside corners can be treated with simple butt joints; otherwise, coped joints are

required. Outside corners should be treated with miter joints, just as if installing baseboard—only upside down. Whenever possible, use screws to fasten the frieze to the wall studs and top plate because they provide more strength and less trauma to the wall than nails. Locate the screws where they will be covered by the next layer of molding, and use nails at those spots that will be exposed.

If your design requires further blocking, install it next. The specific configuration will depend on the moldings you have chosen. Often 2x4 stock can be ripped at the required angle to form continuous backing for a crown or bed molding. Nail or screw the backer to the frieze board. For those situations that demand blocking on the ceiling, methods of fastening can be a problem. On those walls that run perpendicular to ceiling joists, you can use nails or long screws for fastening. However, on walls parallel with the joists, there are often no framing members where you need them. The easiest solution is to get an assistant to help hold the blocking in place on the ceiling, and then drill pilot holes for screws through the blocking and into the drywall surface. Then remove the blocking to install spiral anchors in the pilot holes in the ceiling. You can then replace the blocking, using long screws to attach it.

Place marks on the frieze to act as guides in positioning the next layer of molding. Install that layer, nailing it to the frieze and appropriate backing. Proceed with each layer in similar fashion until the cornice is complete.

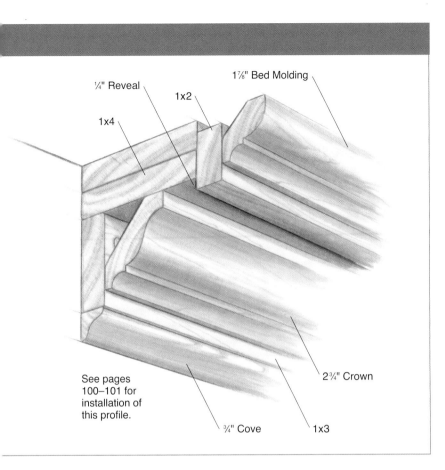

¼" Reveal

1x4

1x2

1⅞" Bed Molding

2¾" Crown

¾" Cove

1x3

See pages 100–101 for installation of this profile.

Beamed & Coffered Ceilings

Although they appear to require a high degree of skill, the assembly of a beamed ceiling is no more complex than that of a built-up cornice—in fact, many of the techniques are identical. A ceiling beam usually consists of a long U-shaped structure that is fastened to strategically located blocking on the ceiling. Beams run parallel with one another and can be spaced evenly or irregularly across a room. Rooms with tall ceilings can generally tolerate larger beams and closer spacing than rooms with lower ceilings. This type of treatment is not limited to rooms with flat ceilings; some of the most dramatic applications of a beamed ceiling are found in spaces with soaring cathedral ceilings. You can orient beams parallel with the rafters or position them so that they run parallel with the ridgeboard to suggest structural purlins.

Coffered ceilings add another level of complexity to the mix. Coffers are recessed areas on a ceiling that are the result of intersecting beams, turning the ceiling surface into a virtual grid. Most often, coffers are square or rectangular, but they can be diamond shaped as well—if the beams run diagonally across a room. The ceiling surface of a coffer can be painted, wallpapered, or covered with boards or veneered panels. This treatment is most appropriate in the more formal rooms of a house, such as a library or dining room.

Beam Materials. Like all interior trim, beamed and coffered ceilings can be constructed using either paint- or stain-grade materials. Pine and poplar are the logical choices for work that will be painted, as they are easy to work and are relatively inexpensive. If painted the same color as the ceiling, the beams become more restrained details, and if given a complementary or contrasting color, they become dominant features in the room. Otherwise, native hardwood species such as oak, cherry, maple, and walnut are popular choices—each contributing its own particular character and associations. Oak makes a strong statement in a room; it accepts stain well, and draws your attention with bold open-grain patterns. Cherry and maple are more subtle choices, contributing warmth and character without overpowering other architectural features. Walnut is associated with elegance and formality; it is a good choice for a more formal public room.

Coffered ceilings are usually ornamental, but they remind us of an earlier, more substantial type of design.

Installing a Beamed Ceiling

Study our drawings, below, to consider some options for ceiling beam construction. Once you have decided on a design, draw a full-scale cross section of a typical beam so that you have a clear plan indicating the sizes of each required part, including the blocking. As an example, if your beam is to be 5 inches wide, you can use 2x4 stock for the interior blocking. Whether your beams are 5 inches or some other width, nominal 2-by material is best to use for blocking because it provides a full 1½ inches of nailing surface for hanging the beams. You can always rip the material to an odd width if the stock size does not suit your plan. If you use ¾-inch-thick stock to construct the beams, the edge of the blocking must be located ¾ inch inside the finished beam wall.

Beam Locations. In planning the locations of beams, it is helpful to note the direction and location of the ceiling joists in the room. Use an electronic stud finder to locate the joists, and place a light pencil mark on the ceiling, adjacent to the wall, to indicate the centerline of each joist. If your beams will run perpendicular to the ceiling joists, your task will be simple—you can screw the blocking directly to each joist. If the beams will run parallel with the joists, you can either decide to locate each beam directly under a joist, use spiral anchors to accept screws, or open the ceiling to install solid blocking between the joists to carry the beams. Unless your beams

are to be extremely large and heavy, tearing into the ceiling should not be necessary—spiral anchors or toggle bolts are easy to use and will support the weight of a decorative beam.

In most cases, it is easiest to construct the beams in a workshop (or any spare room), and install them in one piece or in sections. Then you can apply molding at the ceiling and wall joints, if that is part of your design. It is also possible to build them in place—although the job becomes much more awkward because you must work overhead.

Beam Designs. Beams can be built using several different techniques to join the sides to the bottom. The simplest way is to use butt joints and glue and nail the parts together. This system can be used whether the bottom is recessed from the sides or held flush. Of course, you can use joining plates to align and reinforce the joints. If you use plates, you can still nail the parts, but if you have enough clamps, it is possible to eliminate the nails and the need to fill all those extra holes. Miters are also an option for these joints, however it is quite challenging to fashion a tight joint over the long distances required for a beam, and a less than perfect miter is not an attractive detail.

If you would like a beam to run along a wall, the most common treatment is to construct a partial beam that is approximately half as wide as the beams in the rest of the room. This is a detail that can be used both parallel with the rest of the beams in the room and, on the perpendicular

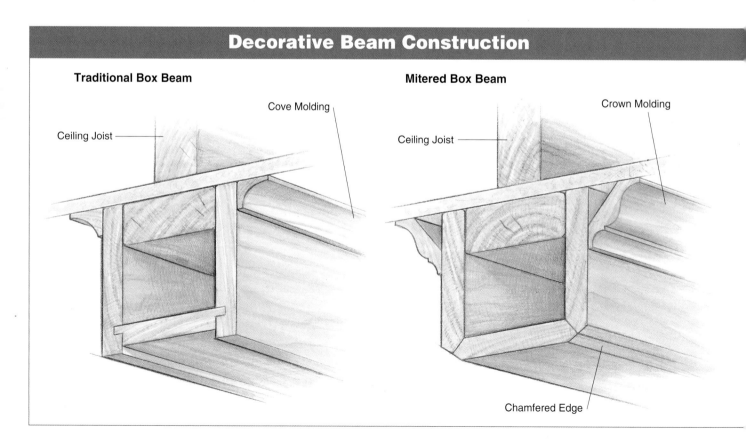

Decorative Beam Construction

Traditional Box Beam

Cove Molding

Ceiling Joist

Mitered Box Beam

Crown Molding

Ceiling Joist

Chamfered Edge

walls, as a way to resolve the intersection of the beams with the wall.

Termination Points. While in the planning stages of your job, give some thought to how you plan to treat the intersection of the beam ends with the wall surface. You can, of course, just let the beams die into the drywall. However, another option, and one that provides some distinct advantages, is to mount a frieze along the wall to accept the beams. If you size the frieze to be wider than the depth of the beams, it can provide a nice, clean transition between the elements. It also provides you with an easier installation by removing the necessity of fitting the beams tightly between the drywall surfaces. You can also use the partial beams, discussed above, as a way to treat the beam ends. These provide a convenient way of ending the beams and create the illusion that the deeper partial beams are supporting those that die into them.

Begin your installation by laying out the position of the blocking for the beams, including partial beams. Place light pencil marks on the ceiling surface, adjacent to each end wall, to indicate the outside edges of each piece of blocking; then strike chalk lines between the marks. Cut the blocking to length; then have an assistant help you to hold it in place along the chalk lines while you drill pilot holes for screws through both blocking and ceiling. If necessary, install spiral anchors in the pilot holes. Screw the blocking to either the ceiling joists or anchors. Repeat the process at each beam location.

Stagger Joints. Take careful measurements for the length of each beam because room dimensions can vary, and then rip and crosscut the parts to size. If you plan to assemble the beams in sections, rather than full length, lay out the joints in sides and bottom so that they are staggered. This will allow you to easily join the sections on site into a continuous straight unit. For a design that includes joining plates, lay out the location of the slots, and cut them using the plate joiner. Assemble the beams in the longest manageable sections using glue, joining plates, and nails, as appropriate.

If your plan includes either a frieze or partial beams as end details, begin your installation there. When a crown or other type of ceiling molding will be used along the beams, you can use screws to hold the beams to the blocking, and the screw heads will be covered by the molding. This is a nice option because it provides another level of detail and can also cover gaps between the beam and an uneven ceiling. In addition, the use of screws eliminates the need for pounding against the blocking. If no molding is included in your plan, use finishing nails to mount the beams. For this job, it is best to use a nail gun, as it will easily and quickly sink the fasteners without beating on the blocking, and it allows you to hold the beam in place with one hand while driving nails with the other.

After you hang all the beams, install the ceiling molding. Treat the beams as you would any wall surface, and cope all inside joints where the beams meet the wall.

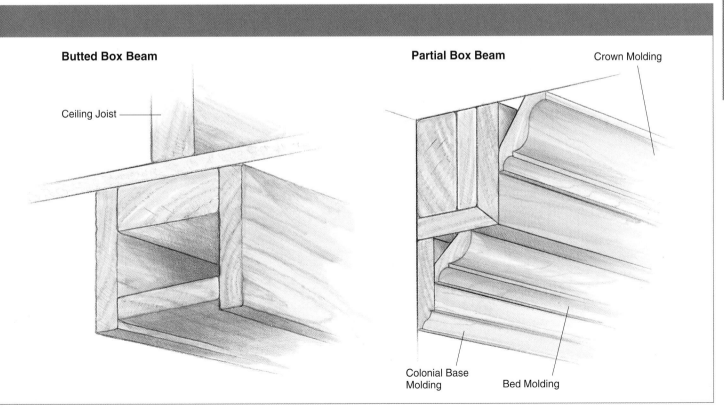

Butted Box Beam

Ceiling Joist

Partial Box Beam

Crown Molding

Colonial Base Molding

Bed Molding

Painted Finishes

Because paint is an opaque coating, it makes sense that it is the more forgiving category of finish. You can fill and sand smooth small gaps in joints and defects in the trim surface prior to applying the final coats of paint, and if well executed, they will not be visible. As mentioned in earlier chapters, a painted finish allows you to select from a wider choice of trim materials. You can use finger-jointed or select pine, poplar, MDF, resin, plaster, or polystyrene foam trim elements, and you can mix materials as well. It is important to remember, though, that paint is not an opaque curtain that will hide a poor installation; sloppy, ill-fitting joints and carelessness in implementing your design will still be apparent. And you may be surprised to see how paint will make some problems visible that you do not even notice in the raw wood surface. So do not approach a paint-grade job as an opportunity to relax your high standards of workmanship. Painted finishes, especially those with glossy sheen levels, can telegraph irregularities in a surface much more than you might expect.

Inspect Surfaces. Use a bright light to illuminate the wood surfaces as you inspect them for defects and mill marks. Even though most boards and molding feel rather smooth if you run your hands over the surface, it is common for there to be parallel knife marks left from the manufacturing process. In some cases, these marks are so subtle that a painted finish will make them invisible. But sometimes, they are readily visible and will telegraph through the finish. If you have some doubt as to how the finish will appear, apply a test finish on scrap material. Examine the finished sample in bright light to judge whether the stock requires sanding before applying the paint.

Removing Hammer Marks

Trim that has been hand nailed will usually show some hammer marks from slips or misses when striking nails. Even professional carpenters will occasionally miss the mark, so don't look at this as an inevitable sign of

inexperience. However, you do not want to leave these marks on the wood because they will telegraph through any type of finish and can ruin an otherwise excellent job. Fortunately, it's not hard to eliminate hammer marks and other dents.

First, make sure that the nailhead is properly set about 1/8 inch below the wood surface. Use a small brush to spread water on the surface of the hammer mark. Then place a clean cotton cloth over the dent, and heat the area using a household iron on the highest setting. The heat of the iron will cause the water to turn to steam, swelling the wood fibers and raising the dented area. For severe defects, you might need to repeat the process two or more times. The water will cause tiny fibers in the grain of the wood to stand up. Smooth the raised grain by lightly sanding.

Four types of paint finishes from left to right—flat, eggshell, semigloss, and gloss. They range from matte to shiny.

Removing Dents

1 A hammer mark will stand out on a piece of newly installed trim. This mark will telegraph through the finish.

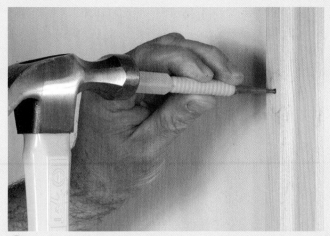

2 Make sure that the nailhead is set about ⅛ in. below the wood surface before beginning the repair.

3 Use a small artist's paintbrush to spread water on the surface of the dent, covering the entire area. Let the water soak in for a minute, and then repeat the application.

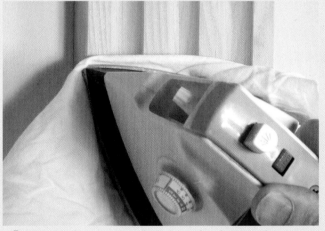

4 Place a clean cotton cloth over the dent, and use a household iron on the highest setting to heat the dented area. The steam will force the wood cells to swell.

5 Use sandpaper and a block to remove the raised grain from the area of the repair.

6 Repeat the process if necessary. The nailhole is now ready for filling.

To fill gaps in inside corners, use a good-quality acrylic latex caulk—one that contains silicone—to fill the spaces in the joint. Remember, though, that caulk is not effective as a remedy for large gaps (those larger than $\frac{1}{16}$ inch). Immediately after you fill a joint, use a wet finger or putty knife to smooth the surface of the caulk and remove excess material. You can also use caulk to fill gaps between trim and the wall or ceiling surface. Fill and tool one joint at a time before the caulk starts to form a skin on its surface.

Filling Nailholes. Because trim relies primarily on nails, and lots of them, to hold the individual elements in place, one of your main concerns will be to fill the holes over the nailheads. If you used a nail gun for installation, the nails should all be properly set. If you have been nailing by hand, go over your work to check that all heads are set. In order for filler to hold well in a hole, the nail should be set about $\frac{1}{8}$ inch below the wood surface.

For paint-grade work, fillers come in two primary types—drying and flexible putty varieties. Of the two types, drying filler will do the better job, but it also requires more work because it must be sanded after application. Drying fillers come in one and two-part formulas. For trimwork, the one-part product is fine and simpler to use. Use a small putty knife or a finger to fill each nailhole. For best results, slightly overfill each hole, because most fillers shrink slightly as they dry. Let the product dry according to the directions on the package; then use sandpaper and a backer block to level the filler flush to the surrounding wood surface. You can also use a drying filler to repair scratches, dents, or natural defects in the wood surface. If the defect is large, you should plan to use two layers of filler, allowing the first layer to dry completely before applying the second.

If you want to use flexible painter's putty to fill nailholes, it is best to prime the wood first. When the primer is dry, lightly sand it to remove any roughness. Knead a golf-ball-size piece of putty until it is soft and pliable; then apply the putty using a knife or your finger. Wipe any excess putty from the surrounding wood surface using a clean rag before applying the first coat of paint.

For filling nailholes in polystyrene molding, the best material to use is drywall compound. Slightly overfill the holes to allow for shrinkage, and when dry, sand off the excess.

Stained finishes, left, allow the natural beauty of the wood to show through.

Use clear lumber, opposite, for any type of clear finish, as defects will become apparent.

Clear or Stained Finishes

Trim that will receive a stained or clear finish requires a different level of care. With a clear finish, even small gaps in joints are hard to hide, so it is inevitable that the installation process will be slower and more demanding. Whether your trim is pine or one of the hardwood species, you should keep in mind that the application of stain will emphasize any defect in the wood surface. Scratches or dents act as magnets for stain, and it will settle in these areas and inevitably draw your eye. Mill marks and cross-grain sanding scratches are also areas that will be accentuated by stain.

Trim Prep. If you're putting a stained or clear finish on your trim, lightly sand the material before you install it to remove many manufacturing defects. As a general rule, 120-grit sandpaper is appropriate for this type of sanding. Use a backing block for the sandpaper whenever possible. Always move the sandpaper parallel with the wood grain. Avoid cross-grain scratches, as they are particularly visible in stained finishes. Power sanders may be useful for sanding flat stock, but if you use an orbital sander, always follow up by hand sanding. Orbital sanders leave small swirl marks on the wood surface, and these can become visible when you apply stain. To remove these marks, use the same-grit paper to give the surface a light sanding, working parallel with the wood grain.

Finishing. You can fill nailholes either before or after you apply the first coat of finish. If you want to use drying filler under a clear unstained finish, you should find one that closely matches the color of the wood. It is best to make up a finished wood sample and use it when selecting the color of the filler because all woods change color when a finish is applied—and various finishes will color the wood differently. Solvent-based finishes tend to lend a warm amber cast to the wood tone, while water-based finishes are clear. Nondrying fillers are available in two types, both intended for use after the finish has been applied. Soft, putty-type fillers are available in a wide variety of colors to match different species and stains. Knead the filler until it is soft, and work it into the holes. Crayon and pencil-style fillers are waxy and quite hard. Rub the stick over the nailhole until it is filled, and then wipe away the excess. Some of these colored fillers will accept a top coat of finish; others are intended for use after the final coat.

For a final touchup after the last coat of finish has cured, use colored markers that are matched to different color finishes. These are handy for small scuffs and scratches that might result from routine life around the house.

glossary

Apron The piece of trim at the *bottom* of a window, below the stool.

Back band Molding used to decorate the outer edges of flat casing. It can also be used as a base cap.

Base cap Molding applied to the top of base trim.

Base shoe Molding used to conceal any variation between the floor and base. It is also used to cover edges of sheet vinyl flooring (when installed without first removing base trim).

Base trim Sometimes called base molding, base trim protects the lower portion of the walls and covers any gaps between the wall and the floor.

Biscuits Football-shaped pieces of compressed wood glued into slots that have been cut into the pieces of stock that will form a joint.

Blocking Wood stock toenailed between or adjacent to studs to give you a solid surface into which to nail the molding.

Built-up trim Several profiles of trim combined to appear as one large piece of molding. Most often it is used as ceiling trim or on the exterior of the home.

Butt joint Two pieces of wood joined at their square cut ends.

Casing The trim that is used to line the inside and outside of a doorway or window frame.

Chair rail Molding installed at a height that protects walls from being damaged by chair backs. It is also used to cover the edges of wainscoting.

Clear grade A grade of lumber or trim that has no knots or other visible defects.

Compound miter A cut that angles in two directions simultaneously.

Coped cut Made with a coping saw, a curved cut is made on a piece of molding with a 45-degree mitered face.

Coped joint A curved cut made across the grain of molding that makes a reverse image of the piece against which it must butt.

Corner guard Trim that protects the outside corners of drywall or plaster in high-traffic areas.

Cove Molding that covers the inside corners between sheets of paneling. It is also used for built-up crown molding.

Crosscut A straight cut that runs across the grain of the wood. Because the grain of trim runs along the length of the piece, a crosscut would be made across the width of the trim.

Crown Molding that is used for a dramatic effect at the juncture of walls and ceilings.

Half-lap miter joint A joint that combines miter, cope, and butt cuts. Half-lap miters are used for moldings with full, rounded-over tops.

Jamb The inside surfaces of a window or door opening.

Miter cut A straight cross-grain cut made at an angle other than 90 degrees to join two pieces of wood.

Mitered return Used to continue the profile of trim back to the wall when the trim does not meet another piece of trim.

Miter joint A corner joint formed by cutting the ends of two pieces of lumber at an equal angle—often 45 degrees.

Molding Thin strips of wood that have a profile created by cutting and shaping.

Mullion casing Center trim that is used between two or more closely spaced windows.

Paint-grade trim Trim made of many small pieces of wood joined together into one long piece, using glue and interlocking joinery called finger joints.

Picture molding Molding used to hang metal hooks to suspend paintings and wall hangings, so there is no need to put holes in the wall.

Plumb Vertically straight, in relation to a horizontally level surface.

Reveal Amount of the jamb (usually ⅛ to ³⁄₁₆ inch) that is allowed to show at the edges of the casing of a window or door.

Rigid polyurethane molding Trim that is extruded into various profiles and sizes. It is lightweight, stable, and paintable.

S4S Stands for "surfaced four sides." Designates dimension lumber that has been planed on all sides.

Sash The framework into which window glass is set. Double-hung windows have an upper and a lower sash.

Scarf joint A 45-degree miter cut across the grain that is used to join lengths of trim end to end.

Screen molding Half-round or flat molding used to protect the cut edges of screening nailed to a wood screen door.

Shelf edging Trim that covers the exposed edges of plywood or particleboard casework and shelving.

Shims Thin wood wedges (often cedar shingles) used for tightening the fit between pieces, such as filling the gap between the window frame and rough-opening sill when installing a window.

Stool The piece of window trim that provides a stop for a lower sash and extends the sill into the room.

Stops Narrow strips of wood nailed to the head and side jambs of doors and windows to prevent a door from swinging too far when it closes and to keep the window sash in line.

Stud Vertical member of a frame wall, usually placed at each end and every 16 inches on center.

Trim General term for any wood used in a house that is not structural lumber. Also, ornamental enhancements that improve the appearance of buildings, both exterior and interior. Includes plain and shaped members.

Wainscoting cap Molding used to cover the exposed end grain on solid or paneled wood wainscoting.

Wainscoting Paneling, paint, fabric wallcovering or other material applied to the lower half of an interior wall.

index

index

photo credits

All tool and how-to shots by Neal Barrett/CH, Gary David Gold/CH, Brian C. Nieves/CH, H. Howard Hudgins, Jr./CH & John Parsekian/CH, unless otherwise noted.

page 1: Mark Lohman, design: Lynn Pries Designs page 3: top davidduncanlivingston.com; bottom Carolyn L. Bates Photography, design: Milford Cushman, The Cushman Design Group page 5: top davidduncanlivingston.com; bottom Tria Giovan Photography page 6: all davidduncanlivingston.com page 7: left & top right davidduncanlivingston.com; bottom right Rob Melnychuk page 8: all davidduncanlivingston.com page 9: top & bottom right davidduncanlivingston.com; bottom left Tria Giovan Photography page 10: top left Tony Giammarino/Giammarino & Dworkin, architect: Fransis Fleetwood; top right davidduncanlivingston.com; bottom Tony Giammarino/Giammarino & Dworkin, design: Beth Scherr Designs page 12: Jessie Walker page 13: davidduncanlivingston.com page 14: Carolyn L. Bates Photography, design: H.R. Thurgate & Sons, LLC page 17: Tony Giammarino/Giammarino & Dworkin, architect: William Darwin Prillaman & Associates page 18: Brian Vanden Brink, architect: John Morris page 19: top Tony Giammarino/Giammarino & Dworkin, design: Marge Thomas; bottom Brian Vanden Brink, architect: Jack Silverio page 20: courtesy of Fypon page 23: Jessie Walker page 42: top left Gary David Gold/CH; right Neal Barrett/CH; bottom left Rob Melnychuk page 51: Rob Melnychuk page 55: Brian Vanden Brink, design: Martin Moore page 56: Gary David Gold/CH page 63: top Tria Giovan Photography; bottom K. Rice/H. Armstrong Roberts page 64: left Mark Lohman, design: Lynn Pries Designs; bottom right Gary David Gold/CH page 69: left Gary David Gold/CH; right davidduncanlivingston.com pages 74–76: all Gary David Gold/CH page 78: Tria Giovan Photography page 90: top left davidduncanlivingston.com; bottom Ivy Moriber, design: Keith Mazzi, DiSalvo Interiors page 91: all Gary David Gold/CH page 98: bottom Jessie Walker, design: Cynthia Muni page 103: Jessie Walker page 108: Brian Vanden Brink page 109: Carolyn L. Bates, design: Milford Cushman, The Cushman Design Group

Shaz

Dee Dee

Billie

May

Index

Photographer Joey Toller • Stylist Kim Hargreaves • Hair & Make-up Wendy Sadd • Model Julie Smyth

DESIGN NUMBER 1

CAT

KIM HARGREAVES

YARN
Rowan Big Wool

		XS	S	M	L	XL	
To fit bust		81	86	91	97	102	cm
		32	34	36	38	40	in
A Smoky	007	5	5	6	6	7	x100gm
B White Hot	001	1	1	1	1	1	x100gm
C Sherbet Lime	002	1	1	1	1	1	x100gm

NEEDLES
1 pair 15mm (US 19) needles

ZIP – 42 cm (16 in) open-ended zip

TENSION
7½ sts and 10 rows to 10 cm measured over stocking stitch using 15mm (US 19) needles.

BACK
Cast on 31 (33: 35: 37: 39) sts using 15mm (US 19) needles and yarn A.
Work in garter st for 6 rows, ending with a WS row.
Beg with a K row, cont in st st as folls:
Work 2 rows, ending with a WS row.
Dec 1 st at each end of next and foll 4th row.
27 (29: 31: 33: 35) sts.
Work 5 rows, ending with a WS row.

Inc 1 st at each end of next and every foll 4th row until there are 33 (35: 37: 39: 41) sts.
Cont straight until back measures 32 cm, ending with a WS row.
Shape raglan armholes
Cast off 2 sts at beg of next 2 rows.
29 (31: 33: 35: 37) sts.
Join in yarn B.
Using yarn B, work 2 rows dec 1 st at each end of first (both: both: both: both) rows.
27 (27: 29: 31: 33) sts.
Join in yarn C.
Using yarn C, work 2 rows, dec 1 st at each end of first row. 25 (25: 27: 29: 31) sts.
Break off yarn C.
Using yarn B, work 2 rows, dec 1 st at each end of first row. 23 (23: 25: 27: 29) sts.
Break off yarn B and cont using yarn A only.
Dec 1 st at each end of next and every foll alt row until 9 (9: 9: 11: 11) sts rem.
Work 1 row, ending with a WS row. Cast off.

LEFT FRONT
Cast on 16 (17: 18: 19: 20) sts using 15mm (US 19) needles and yarn A.
Work in garter st for 6 rows, ending with a WS row.
Next row (RS): Knit.
Next row: K1, P to end.
These 2 rows set the sts – front opening edge st worked as a K st on every row with all other sts in st st.
Keeping sts correct, cont as folls:
Dec 1 st at beg of next and foll 4th row.
14 (15: 16: 17: 18) sts.
Work 5 rows, ending with a WS row.
Inc 1 st at beg of next and every foll 4th row until there are 17 (18: 19: 20: 21) sts.
Cont straight until left front matches back to beg of raglan armhole shaping, ending with a WS row.
Shape raglan armhole
Cast off 2 sts at beg of next row.
15 (16: 17: 18: 19) sts.
Work 1 row.
Join in yarn B.
Using yarn B, work 2 rows dec 1 st at raglan armhole edge of first (both: both: both: both) rows. 14 (14: 15: 16: 17) sts.
Join in yarn C.
Using yarn C, work 2 rows, dec 1 st at raglan armhole edge of first row. 13 (13: 14: 15: 16) sts.
Break off yarn C.

Using yarn B, work 2 rows, dec 1 st at raglan armhole edge of first row. 12 (12: 13: 14: 15) sts.
Break off yarn B and cont using yarn A only.
Medium and extra large sizes
Work 2 rows dec 1 st at raglan armhole edge of first row. - (-: 12: -: 14) sts.
All sizes
Shape front slope
Dec 1 st at each end of next and every foll alt row until 2 sts rem.
Dec 1 st at raglan armhole edge only on foll alt row. 1 st.
Next row (WS): P1 and fasten off.

RIGHT FRONT
Cast on 16 (17: 18: 19: 20) sts using 15mm (US 19) needles and yarn A.
Work in garter st for 6 rows, ending with a WS row.
Next row (RS): Knit.
Next row: P to last st, K1.
These 2 rows set the sts – front opening edge st worked as a K st on every row with all other sts in st st. Keeping sts correct, cont as folls:
Dec 1 st at end of next and foll 4th row.
14 (15: 16: 17: 18) sts.
Complete to match left front, reversing shapings.

SLEEVES
Cast on 19 (19: 21: 21: 23) sts using 15mm (US 19) needles and yarn A.
Work in garter st for 6 rows, ending with a WS row.
Beg with a K row, cont in st st, shaping sides by inc 1 st at each end of 5th and foll 10th row, then on every foll 8th row until there are 27 (27: 29: 29: 31) sts. Cont straight until sleeve measures 44 (44: 45: 45: 45) cm, ending with a WS row.
Shape raglan
Cast off 2 sts at beg of next 2 rows.
23 (23: 25: 25: 27) sts.
Join in yarn B.
Using yarn B, work 2 rows dec 1 st at each end of first row. 21 (21: 23: 23: 25) sts.
Join in yarn C.
Using yarn C, work 2 rows, dec 1 st at each end of first row. 19 (19: 21: 21: 23) sts.
Break off yarn C.
Using yarn B, work 2 rows, dec 1 st at each end of first row. 17 (17: 19: 19: 21) sts.
Break off yarn B and cont using yarn A only.
Dec 1 st at each end of next and every foll alt row until 5 sts rem.

Work 1 row, ending with a WS row.

Left sleeve only

Next row (RS): K2tog, K1, cast off rem 2 sts.
Rejoin yarn to rem 2 sts with WS facing.

Right sleeve only

Cast off 2 sts at beg and dec 1 st at end of next row. 2 sts.

Both sleeves

Next row (WS): P2tog and fasten off.

MAKING UP

PRESS all pieces as described on the info page.
Join raglan seams using back stitch, or mattress stitch if preferred.

Collar

Cast on 2 sts using 15mm (US 19) needles and yarn A.
Beg with a RS row, cont in garter st as folls:
Inc 1 st at end of next and every foll alt row until there are 12 sts.
Work a further 25 (25: 27: 29: 31) rows, ending with a WS row.
Dec 1 st at end of next and every foll alt row until 2 sts rem.
Next row (WS): K2tog and fasten off.
Sew shaped edge of collar to neck edge, easing in slight fullness. Insert zip into front opening. See information page for finishing instructions.

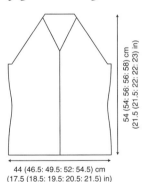

44 (46.5: 49.5: 52: 54.5) cm
(17.5: 18.5: 19.5: 20.5: 21.5) in

54 (54: 56: 56: 58) cm
(21.5 (21.5: 22: 22: 23) in

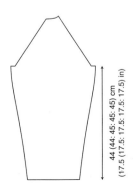

44 (44: 45: 45: 45) cm
(17.5 (17.5: 17.5: 17.5: 17.5) in

TRUDI

KIM HARGREAVES

YARN

Rowan Big Wool

	XS	S	M	L	XL	
To fit bust	81	86	91	97	102	cm
	32	34	36	38	40	in
	3	3	3	4	4	x 100gm

(photographed in Black 008)

NEEDLES

1 pair 15mm (US 19) needles

TENSION

7½ sts and 10 rows to 10 cm measured over stocking stitch using 15mm (US 19) needles.

BACK and FRONT (both alike)

Cast on 28 (30: 32: 34: 36) sts using 15mm (US 19) needles.
Beg with a K row, cont in st st as folls:
Work 4 rows, ending with a WS row.
Dec 1 st at each end of next and foll 4th row. 24 (26: 28: 30: 32) sts.
Work 3 (5: 5: 5: 5) rows, ending with a WS row.
Inc 1 st at each end of next and every foll 6th row until there are 30 (32: 34: 36: 38) sts.
Cont straight until work measures 28 (29: 29: 30: 30) cm, ending with a WS row.

Shape armholes

Cast off 2 (2: 2: 2: 3) sts at beg of next 2 rows. 26 (28: 30: 32: 32) sts.
Dec 1 st at each end of next 2 (2: 3: 3: 3) rows. 22 (24: 24: 26: 26) sts.
Cont straight until armhole measures 20 (20: 21: 21: 22) cm, ending with a WS row.

Shape shoulders

Cast off 1 (2: 2: 2: 2) sts at beg of next 2 rows, then 2 sts at beg of foll 2 rows.
16 (16: 16: 18: 18) sts.
Break yarn and leave sts on a holder.

MAKING UP

PRESS all pieces as described on the information page.
Join right shoulder seam using back stitch, or mattress stitch if preferred.

Neckband

With RS facing and 15mm (US 19) needles, knit across 16 (16: 16: 18: 18) sts from front holder, then 16 (16: 16: 18: 18) sts from back holder. 32 (32: 32: 36: 36) sts.
Beg with a P row, work in st st for 4 rows.
Cast off.
See information page for finishing instructions.

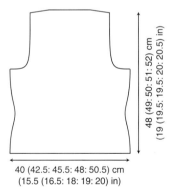

40 (42.5: 45.5: 48: 50.5) cm
(15.5 (16.5: 18: 19: 20) in)

48 (49: 50: 51: 52) cm
(19 (19.5: 19.5: 20: 20.5) in)

Shaz

Kim Hargreaves

YARN

Rowan Big Wool

	XS	S	M	L	XL
To fit bust	81	86	91	97	102 cm
	32	34	36	38	40 in
	8	8	9	9	10 x100gm

(photographed in Merry Berry 006)

NEEDLES

1 pair 15mm (US 19) needles
Cable needle

TENSION

7½ sts and 10 rows to 10 cm measured over stocking stitch using 15mm (US 19) needles.

SPECIAL ABBREVIATIONS

C6F = Cable 6 front Slip next 3 sts onto cable needle and leave at front of work, K3, then K3 from cable needle.
C6B = Cable 6 back Slip next 3 sts onto cable needle and leave at back of work, K3, then K3 from cable needle.

BACK

Cast on 44 (46: 48: 50: 52) sts using 15mm (US 19) needles.

Row 1 (RS): P0 (0: 1: 0: 0), K1 (2: 2: 0: 1), ★P2, K2, rep from ★ to last 3 (0: 1: 2: 3) sts, P2 (0: 1: 2: 2), K1 (0: 0: 0: 1).
Row 2: K0 (0: 1: 0: 0), P1 (2: 2: 0: 1), ★K2, P2, rep from ★ to last 3 (0: 1: 2: 3) sts, K2 (0: 1: 2: 2), P1 (0: 0: 0: 1).
These 2 rows form rib.
Work in rib for a further 8 rows, ending with a WS row.
Beg with a P row, cont in rev st st until back measures 45 (46: 46: 47: 47) cm, end with a WS row.

Shape armholes

Cast off 4 sts at beg of next 2 rows.
36 (38: 40: 42: 44) sts.
Cont straight until armhole measures 25 (25: 26: 26: 27) cm, ending with a WS row.

Shape shoulders and back neck

Cast off 3 (4: 4: 4: 5) sts at beg of next 2 rows.
30 (30: 32: 34: 34) sts.
Next row (RS): Cast off 3 (4: 4: 4: 5) sts, P until there are 7 (6: 7: 8: 7) sts on right needle and turn, leaving rem sts on a holder.
Work each side of neck separately.
Cast off 3 sts at beg of next row.
Cast off rem 4 (3: 4: 5: 4) sts.
With RS facing, rejoin yarn to rem sts, cast off centre 10 sts **firmly**, P to end.
Work to match first side, reversing shapings.

FRONT

Cast on 48 (50: 52: 54: 56) sts using 15mm (US 19) needles.
Row 1 (RS): P0 (0: 1: 0: 0), K1 (2: 2: 0: 1), (P2, K2) 4 (4: 4: 5: 5) times, P1, K12, P1, (K2, P2) 4 (4: 4: 5: 5) times, K1 (2: 2: 0: 1), P0 (0: 1: 0: 0).
Row 2: K0 (0: 1: 0: 0), P1 (2: 2: 0: 1), (K2, P2) 4 (4: 4: 5: 5) times, K1, P12, K1, (P2, K2) 4 (4: 4: 5: 5) times, P1 (2: 2: 0: 1), K0 (0: 1: 0: 0).
Rep these 2 rows 3 times more.
Row 9 (RS): P0 (0: 1: 0: 0), K1 (2: 2: 0: 1), (P2, K2) 4 (4: 4: 5: 5) times, P1, C6B, C6F, P1, (K2, P2) 4 (4: 4: 5: 5) times, K1 (2: 2: 0: 1), P0 (0: 1: 0: 0).
Row 10: As row 2.
Cont in cable patt as folls:
Row 1 (RS): P18 (19: 20: 21: 22), K12, P18 (19: 20: 21: 22).
Row 2: K18 (19: 20: 21: 22), P12, K18 (19: 20: 21: 22).
Rows 3 to 6: As rows 1 and 2, twice.
Row 7: P18 (19: 20: 21: 22), C6B, C6F, P18 (19: 20: 21: 22).
Row 8: As row 2.
These 8 rows form cable patt.
Cont in patt until front matches back to beg of armhole shaping, ending with a WS row.

Shape armholes

Cast off 4 sts at beg of next 2 rows.
40 (42: 44: 46: 48) sts.
Cont straight until 6 rows less have been worked than on back to start of shoulder shaping, ending with a WS row.

Shape neck

Next row (RS): P14 (15: 16: 17: 18) and turn, leaving rem sts on a holder.
Work each side of neck separately.
Dec 1 st at neck edge on next 4 rows.
10 (11: 12: 13: 14) sts.
Work 1 row, ending with a WS row.

Shape shoulder

Cast off 3 (4: 4: 4: 5) sts at beg of next and foll alt row.
Work 1 row.
Cast off rem 4 (3: 4: 5: 4) sts.
With RS facing, slip centre 12 sts onto a holder, rejoin yarn to rem sts, P to end.
Work to match first side, reversing shapings.

SLEEVES (both alike)

Cast on 26 sts using 15mm (US 19) needles.
Row 1 (RS): P2, ★K2, P2, rep from ★ to end.
Row 2: K2, ★P2, K2, rep from ★ to end.
These 2 rows form rib.
Work in rib for a further 8 rows, inc 1 st at each end of 7th of these rows and ending with a WS row. 28 sts.
Beg with a P row, cont in rev st st, shaping sides by inc 1 st at each end of 5th (5th: 3rd: 3rd: 3rd) and every foll 6th (6th: 4th: 4th: 4th) row to 36 (36: 32: 32: 38) sts, then on every foll 8th (8th: 6th: 6th: 6th) row until there are 38 (38: 40: 40: 42) sts.
Cont straight until sleeve measures 51 (51: 52: 52: 52) cm, ending with a WS row.
Cast off.

MAKING UP

PRESS all pieces as described on the info page.
Join right shoulder seam using back stitch, or mattress stitch if preferred.
Neckband
With RS facing and 15mm (US 19) needles, pick up and knit 7 sts down left side of neck, patt

across 12 sts from front holder, pick up and knit 7 sts up right side of neck, then 16 sts from back. 42 sts.

Row 1 (WS): (P2, K2) 5 times, P2, K1, patt 12 sts, K1, P2, K2, P2.

Row 2: K2, P2, K2, P1, patt 12 sts, P1, K2, (P2, K2) 5 times.

Rep last 2 rows for 10 cm.

Cast off in patt, dec 6 sts across top of cable.

See information page for finishing instructions, setting in sleeves using the square set-in method.

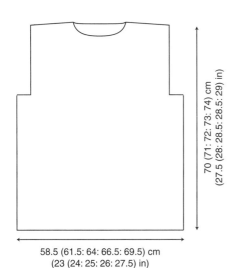

70 (71: 72: 73: 74) cm
(27.5 (28: 28.5: 28.5: 29) in)

58.5 (61.5: 64: 66.5: 69.5) cm
(23 (24: 25: 26: 27.5) in)

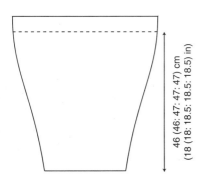

46 (46: 47: 47: 47) cm
(18 (18: 18.5: 18.5: 18.5) in)

DESIGN NUMBER 4

CHRISSIE

KIM HARGREAVES

YARN

Rowan Big Wool

	XS	S	M	L	XL	
To fit bust	81	86	91	97	102	cm
	32	34	36	38	40	in
	8	8	9	9	10	x100gm

(photographed in Smoky 007)

NEEDLES

1 pair 15mm (US 19) needles
1 pair 10mm (UK 000) (US 15) needles

BUTTONS - 6

TENSION

7½ sts and 10 rows to 10 cm measured over stocking stitch using 15mm (US 19) needles.

BACK

Cast on 38 (40: 42: 44: 46) sts using 15mm (US 19) needles.

Work in garter st for 8 rows, ending with a WS row.

Beg with a K row, cont in st st as folls:

Work 18 rows, ending with a WS row.

Dec 1 st at each end of next and foll 6th row, then on foll 4th row. 32 (34: 36: 38: 40) sts.

Work 3 rows, ending with a WS row.

Inc 1 st at each end of next and every foll 4th row until there are 38 (40: 42: 44: 46) sts.

Cont straight until back measures 54 cm, ending with a WS row.

Shape raglan armholes

Cast off 2 sts at beg of next 2 rows.

34 (36: 38: 40: 42) sts.

Medium and extra large sizes

Next row (RS): P2, K2tog, K to last 4 sts, K2tog tbl, P2.

Next row: K2, P2tog tbl, P to last 4 sts, P2tog, K2. – (–: 34: –: 38) sts.

All sizes

Next row (RS): P2, K2tog, K to last 4 sts, K2tog tbl, P2.

Next row: K2, P to last 2 sts, K2.

Rep last 2 rows 10 (11: 10: 12: 11) times more.

Cast off rem 12 (12: 12: 14: 14) sts.

POCKET LININGS (make 2)

Cast on 11 sts using 15mm (US 19) needles.

Beg with a K row, work in st st for 14 rows.

Break yarn and leave sts on a holder.

LEFT FRONT

Cast on 23 (24: 25: 26: 27) sts using 15mm (US 19) needles.

Work in garter st for 8 rows, ending with a WS row.

Next row (RS): Knit.

Next row: K5, P to end.

These 2 rows set the sts – front opening edge 5 sts in garter st with all other sts in st st.

Keeping sts correct as set, work a further 14 rows, ending with a WS row.

Place pocket

Next row (RS): K3 (4: 4: 5: 5), slip next 11 sts onto a holder and, in their place, K across 11 sts of first pocket lining, K9 (9: 10: 10: 11).

Work 1 row, ending with a WS row.

Dec 1 st at beg of next and foll 6th row, then on foll 4th row. 20 (21: 22: 23: 24) sts.

Work 3 rows, ending with a WS row.

Inc 1 st at beg of next and every foll 4th row until there are 23 (24: 25: 26: 27) sts.

Cont straight until left front matches back to beg of armhole shaping, ending with a WS row.

Shape raglan armhole

Cast off 2 sts at beg of next row.

21 (22: 23: 24: 25) sts.

Work 1 row.

Medium and extra large sizes

Next row (RS): P2, K2tog, K to end.

Next row: K5, P to last 4 sts, P2tog, K2.

– (–: 21: –: 23) sts

All sizes

Next row (RS): P2, K2tog, K to end.

Next row: K5, P to last 2 sts, K2.

Rep last 2 rows 5 (6: 5: 7: 6) times more, and then first of these 2 rows again, ending with a RS row. 14 (14: 14: 15: 15) sts.

Shape neck

Next row (WS): Patt 6 (6: 6: 7: 7) sts and slip these sts onto a holder, P to last 2 sts, K2. 8 sts.

Next row: P2, K2tog, K2, K2tog.

Next row: P2tog, P2, K2.

Next row: P2, s1, K2tog, psso.

Next row: P1, K2.

Next row: P3tog.

Next row: K1 and fasten off.

Mark positions for 6 buttons along left front opening edge – first to come in 21st row, last to come just below neck shaping and rem 4 buttons evenly spaced between.

RIGHT FRONT

Cast on 23 (24: 25: 26: 27) sts using 15mm (US 19) needles.

Work in garter st for 8 rows, ending with a WS row.

Next row (RS): Knit.

Next row: P to last 5 sts, K5.

These 2 rows set the sts – front opening edge 5 sts in garter st with all other sts in st st.

Keeping sts correct as set, work a further 10 rows, ending with a WS row.

Next row (buttonhole row) (RS): K1, K2tog, yfwd, K to end.

Making a further 5 buttonholes in this way to correspond with positions marked on left front for buttons and noting that no further reference will be made to buttonholes, cont as folls:

Work a further 3 rows, ending with a WS row.

Place pocket

Next row (RS): K9 (9: 10: 10: 11), slip next 11 sts onto a holder and, in their place, K across 11 sts of first pocket lining, K3 (4: 4: 5: 5).

Work 1 row, ending with a WS row.

Dec 1 st at end of next and foll 6th row, then on foll 4th row.

20 (21: 22: 23: 24) sts.

Complete to match left front, reversing shapings.

SLEEVES

Cast on 24 (24: 24: 26: 26) sts using 15mm (US 19) needles.

Work in garter st for 8 rows, ending with a WS row.

Beg with a K row, cont in st st, shaping sides by inc 1 st at each end of 5th and every foll 18th (10th: 10th: 10th: 10th) row until there are 28 (30: 30: 32: 32) sts.

Cont straight until sleeve measures 40 (40: 41: 41: 41) cm, ending with a WS row.

Shape raglan

Cast off 2 sts at beg of next 2 rows.

24 (26: 26: 28: 28) sts.

Next row (RS): P2, K2tog, K to last 4 sts, K2tog tbl, P2.

Next row: K2, P to last 2 sts, K2.

Next row: P2, K to last 2 sts, P2.

Next row: K2, P to last 2 sts, K2.

Rep last 4 rows once more.

20 (22: 22: 24: 24) sts.

Next row (RS): P2, K2tog, K to last 4 sts, K2tog tbl, P2.

Next row: K2, P to last 2 sts, K2.

Rep last 2 rows 5 (6: 6: 7: 7) times more. 8 sts.

Left sleeve only

Next row (RS): P2, K2tog, K1, cast off rem 3 sts.

Rejoin yarn to rem 4 sts with WS facing and patt to end.

Right sleeve only

Cast off 3 sts at beg and dec 1 st at end of next row. 4 sts.

Work 1 row.

Both sleeves

Cast off rem 4 sts.

MAKING UP

PRESS all pieces as described on the info page. Join raglan seams using back stitch, or mattress stitch if preferred.

Collar

With RS facing and 15mm (US 19) needles, slip 6 (6: 6: 7: 7) sts left on right front holder onto right needle, rejoin yarn and pick up and knit 4 sts up right side of neck, 6 sts from right sleeve, 12 (12: 12: 14: 14) from back, 6 sts from left sleeve, 4 sts down left side of neck, then K across 6 (6: 6: 7: 7) sts left on left front holder.

44 (44: 44: 48: 48) sts.

Work in garter st for 15 rows.

Cast off knitwise.

Belt

Cast on 6 sts using 10mm (US 15) needles.

Work in garter st until belt measures 150 cm.

Cast off.

Pocket tops (both alike)

Slip 11 sts left on pocket holder onto 15mm (US 19) needles and rejoin yarn with RS facing.

Work in garter st for 3 rows.

Cast off knitways (on WS).

See information page for finishing instructions.

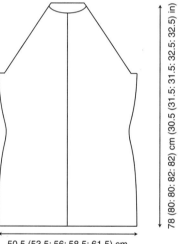

78 (80: 80: 82: 82) cm (30.5 (31.5: 31.5: 32.5: 32.5) in)

50.5 (53.5: 56: 58.5: 61.5) cm (20 (21: 22: 23: 24) in)

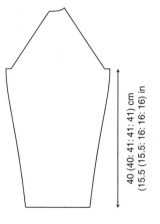

40 (40: 41: 41: 41) cm (15.5 (15.5: 16: 16: 16) in)

DESIGN NUMBER 5

JERRY

KIM HARGREAVES

YARN
Rowan Big Wool

	XS	S	M	L	XL	
To fit bust	81	86	91	97	102	cm
	32	34	36	38	40	in
	8	8	8	9	9	x100gm

(photographed in White Hot 001)

NEEDLES
1 pair 15mm (US 19) needles

TENSION
7½ sts and 10 rows to 10 cm measured over stocking stitch using 15mm (US 19) needles.

BACK
Cast on 41 (43: 45: 47: 49) sts using 15mm (US 19) needles.
Row 1 (RS): P2 (0: 1: 2: 0), *K1, P2, rep from * to last 0 (1: 2: 0: 1) sts, K0 (1: 1: 0: 1), P0 (0: 1: 0: 0).
Row 2: K2 (0: 1: 2: 0), *P1, K2, rep from * to last 0 (1: 2: 0: 1) sts, P0 (1: 1: 0: 1), K0 (0: 1: 0: 0).
These 2 rows form rib.
Work in rib for a further 12 rows, ending with a WS row.
Beg with a K row, cont in st st until back measures 48 cm, ending with a WS row.

Shape raglan armholes
Cast off 2 sts at beg of next 2 rows.
37 (39: 41: 43: 45) sts.
Next row (RS): P2, K2tog, K to last 4 sts, K2tog tbl, P2.
Next row: K2, P2tog tbl, P to last 4 sts, P2tog, K2.
Rep last 2 rows 1 (1: 2: 2: 3) times more.
29 (31: 29: 31: 29) sts.
Next row (RS): P2, K2tog, K to last 4 sts, K2tog tbl, P2.
Next row: K2, P to last 2 sts, K2.
Rep last 2 rows 8 (9: 8: 9: 8) times more.
Cast off rem 11 sts.

FRONT
Work as given for back until 17 sts rem in raglan shaping. Work 1 row, ending with a WS row.
Shape neck
Next row (RS): P2, K2tog, K1 and turn, leaving rem sts on a holder.
Work each side of neck separately.
Next row: P2tog, K2. 3 sts.
Next row: P3tog.
Next row: K1 and fasten off.
With RS facing, rejoin yarn to rem sts and cont as folls:
Next row (RS): cast off 7 sts (1 st on right needle, 4 sts rem on left needle), K2tog tbl, P2.
Next row: K2, P2tog. 3 sts.
Next row: P3tog.
Next row: K1 and fasten off.

SLEEVES
Cast on 27 sts using 15mm (US 19) needles.
Row 1 (RS): P1, *K1, P2, rep from * to last 2 sts, K1, P1.
Row 2: K1, *P1, K2, rep from * to last 2 sts, P1, K1.
These 2 rows form rib. Work in rib for a further 12 rows, inc 1 st at each end of 9th of these rows and ending with a WS row. 29 sts.
Beg with a K row, cont in st st, shaping sides by inc 1 st at each end of 9th (7th: 7th: 5th: 5th) and every foll 12th (10th: 10th: 8th: 8th) row until there are 33 (35: 35: 37: 37) sts.
Cont straight until sleeve measures 46 (46: 47: 47: 47) cm, ending with a WS row.
Shape raglan
Cast off 2 sts at beg of next 2 rows.
29 (31: 31: 33: 33) sts.
Next row (RS): P2, K2tog, K to last 4 sts, K2tog tbl, P2.

Next row: K2, P2tog tbl, P to last 4 sts, P2tog, K2. 25 (27: 27: 29: 29) sts.
Next row (RS): P2, K2tog, K to last 4 sts, K2tog tbl, P2.
Next row: K2, P to last 2 sts, K2.
Rep last 2 rows 8 (9: 9: 10: 10) times more. 7 sts.
Left sleeve only
Next row (RS): P2, K2tog, cast off rem 3 sts.
Rejoin yarn to rem 3 sts with WS facing and patt to end.
Right sleeve only
Cast off 3 sts at beg and dec 1 st at end of next row. 3 sts. Work 1 row.
Both sleeves
Cast off rem 3 sts.

MAKING UP
PRESS all pieces as described on the info page.
Join both front and right back raglan seams using back stitch, or mattress stitch if preferred.
Collar
With RS facing and 15mm (US 19) needles, pick up and knit 6 sts from left sleeve, 4 sts down left side of neck, 7 sts from front, 4 sts up right side of neck, 6 sts from right sleeve, then 12 sts from back. 39 sts.

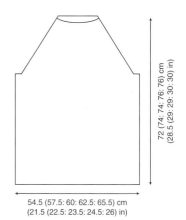

54.5 (57.5: 60: 62.5: 65.5) cm
(21.5 (22.5: 23.5: 24.5: 26) in)

72 (74: 74: 76: 76) cm
(28.5 (29: 29: 30: 30) in)

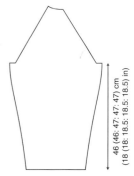

46 (46: 47: 47: 47) cm
(18 (18: 18.5: 18.5: 18.5) in)

Row 1 (WS): P1, *K1, P1, rep from * to end.
Row 2: K1, *P1, K1, rep from * to end.
Rep last 2 rows 3 times more, then row 1 again.
Row 10: Inc in first st, *P1, inc in next st, rep from * to end. 59 sts.
Row 11: P2, *K1, P2, rep from * to end.

Row 12: K2, *P1, K2, rep from * to end.
Rep rows 11 and 12 until collar measures 24 cm from pick-up row.
Cast off in patt.
See information page for finishing instructions, reversing collar seam for turn-back.

MEL

KIM HARGREAVES

YARN
Rowan Big Wool 3 x 100gm
(photographed in White Hot 001)

NEEDLES
1 pair 15mm (US 19) needles

LINING
Piece each of fabric and wadding approx 40 cm by 70 cm.

TENSION
7½ sts and 10 rows to 10 cm measured over stocking stitch using 15mm (US 19) needles.

FINISHED SIZE
Completed bag is approx 25 cm (10 in) wide, 25 cm (10 in) tall and 10 cm (4 in) deep.

SIDES (make 2)
Cast on 4 sts using 15mm (US 19) needles
Break yarn and set these sts to one side.
Cast on 19 sts using 15mm (US 19) needles
Beg with a K row, work in st st for 5 rows.
Shape for side gussets
Next row (WS): Cast on and P 4 sts, P to end, then P across 4 sts set to one side. 27 sts.
Next row: K4, slip next st purlwise (for side gusset fold line), K to last 5 sts, slip next st purlwise (for side gusset fold line), K4.
Next row: Purl.
Rep last 2 rows 11 times more, end with a WS row.
Beg with a K row, work in st st for a further 6 rows.
Cast off.

STRAPS (make 2)
Cast on 9 sts using 15mm (US 19) needles
Row 1 (RS): K2, slip next st purlwise (for fold line), K3, slip next st purlwise (for fold line), K2.
Row 2: Purl.
Rep these 2 rows 17 times more. Cast off.

MAKING UP
PRESS as described on the info page. From fabric, cut two pieces same shape as knitted sides, adding 1 cm seam allowance along side and lower edges and trimming 5 cm off upper (cast-off) edge. From wadding, cut out side shape twice. Sew knitted side pieces together along row end edges and across cast-on edge. Fold bag so that 4 cast-on sts match row end edges of first 5 rows and side/base seams meet, then sew base seam of side gussets. Fold last 6 rows to inside along slipped st fold lines and join row end edges along length. Fold straps along fold lines and join together along length. Sew straps inside top of bag 10 cm apart. Tack wadding in position on WS of lining pieces, then sew up lining pieces in same way as for knitted section, folding 1 cm to inside around upper edge. Slip lining/wadding section inside bag and slip stitch in place around opening edge.

KATE

KIM HARGREAVES

YARN
Rowan Big Wool

		XS	S	M	L	XL	
To fit bust		81	86	91	97	102	cm
		32	34	36	38	40	in
A Merry Berry 006		3	3	3	4	4	x100gm
B Shriek 005		3	3	3	4	4	x100gm

NEEDLES
1 pair 15mm (US 19) needles

ZIP
ZIP – 51 (51: 56: 56: 56) cm open-ended zip

TENSION
7¹/ sts and 10 rows to 10 cm measured over stocking stitch using 15mm (US 19) needles.

BACK
Cast on 31 (33: 35: 37: 39) sts using 15mm (US 19) needles and yarn A.
Row 1 (RS): P0 (1: 2: 0: 1), *K1, P2, rep from * to last 1 (2: 0: 1: 2) sts, K1 (1: 0: 1: 1), P0 (1: 0: 0: 1).
Row 2: K0 (1: 2: 0: 1), *P1, K2, rep from * to last 1 (2: 0: 1: 2) sts, P1 (1: 0: 1: 1), K0 (1: 0: 0: 1).
Rep last 2 rows once more.
Beg with a K row, cont in st st as folls:
Work 2 rows, ending with a WS row.

Join in yarn B.

Using yarn B, work 6 rows **and at the same time** dec 1 st at each end of next and foll 4th row. 27 (29: 31: 33: 35) sts.

Using yarn A, work 6 rows, inc 1 st at each end of 5th of these rows. 29 (31: 33: 35: 37) sts.

Last 12 rows form striped st st (a 12 row repeat of 6 rows using yarn A followed by 6 rows using yarn B) and start side seam shaping.

Keeping striped st st correct, cont as folls:

Inc 1 st at each end of 3rd and foll 4th row. 33 (35: 37: 39: 41) sts.

Work 5 rows, ending after 6 rows using yarn A and with a WS row.

Shape raglan armholes

Keeping striped st st correct, cast off 2 sts at beg of next 2 rows. 29 (31: 33: 35: 37) sts.

Dec 1 st at each end of next 1 (3: 3: 3: 3) rows, then on every foll alt row until 9 (9: 9: 11: 11) sts rem. Work 1 row, ending with a WS row. Cast off.

LEFT FRONT

Cast on 16 (17: 18: 19: 20) sts using 15mm (US 19) needles and yarn A.

Row 1 (RS): P0 (1: 2: 0: 1), ★K1, P2, rep from ★ to last st, K1.

Row 2: K3, ★P1, K2, rep from ★ to last 1 (2: 0: 1: 2) sts, P1 (1: 0: 1: 1), K0 (1: 0: 0: 1).

Rep last 2 rows once more.

Next row (RS): Knit.

Next row: K1, P to end.

These 2 rows set the sts – front opening edge st worked as a K st on every row with all other sts in st st.

Join in yarn B.

Beg with 6 rows using yarn B, now work in stripes as given for back and, keeping sts correct, cont as folls:

Dec 1 st at beg of next and foll 4th row. 14 (15: 16: 17: 18) sts.

Work 5 rows, ending with a WS row.

Inc 1 st at beg of next and every foll 4th row until there are 17 (18: 19: 20: 21) sts.

Work 5 rows, ending with a WS row.

Shape raglan armhole

Keeping stripes correct, cast off 2 sts at beg of next row. 15 (16: 17: 18: 19) sts.

Work 1 row.

Dec 1 st at raglan armhole edge of next 1 (3: 3: 3: 3) rows, then on every foll alt row until 8 (8: 8: 9: 9) sts rem, ending with a RS row.

Shape neck

Cast off 3 (3: 3: 4: 4) sts at beg of next row. 5 sts.

Dec 1 st at neck edge of next 2 rows and at same time dec 1 st at raglan armhole edge on next row. 2 sts.

Dec 1 st at raglan armhole edge of next row.

Next row (WS): P1 and fasten off.

RIGHT FRONT

Cast on 16 (17: 18: 19: 20) sts using 15mm (US 19) needles and yarn A.

Row 1 (RS): ★K1, P2, rep from ★ to last 1 (2: 0: 1: 2) sts, K1 (1: 0: 1: 1), P0 (1: 0: 0: 1).

Row 2: K0 (1: 2: 0: 1), ★P1, K2, rep from ★ to last st, K1.

Rep last 2 rows once more.

Next row (RS): Knit.

Next row: P to last st, K1.

These 2 rows set the sts – front opening edge st worked as a K st on every row with all other sts in st st.

Join in yarn B.

Beg with 6 rows using yarn B, now work in stripes as given for back and, keeping sts correct, cont as folls: Dec 1 st at end of next and foll 4th row. 14 (15: 16: 17: 18) sts.

Complete to match left front, reversing shapings.

SLEEVES

Cast on 19 (19: 21: 21: 23) sts using 15mm (US 19) needles and yarn A.

Row 1 (RS): P0 (0: 1: 1: 2), ★K1, P2, rep from ★ to last 1 (1: 2: 2: 3) sts, K1, P0 (0: 1: 1: 2).

Row 2: K0 (0: 1: 1: 2), ★P1, K2, rep from ★ to last 1 (1: 2: 2: 3) sts, P1, K0 (0: 1: 1: 2).

Rep last 2 rows twice more.

Beg with a K row, work in st st for 2 rows.

Join in yarn B.

Beg with 6 rows using yarn B, now work in striped st st as given for back as folls:

Inc 1 st at each end of 3rd and foll 10th row, then on every foll 8th row until there are 27 (27: 29: 29: 31) sts.

Cont straight until sleeve measures approx 44 cm, ending after 6 rows using yarn A and with a WS row.

Shape raglan

Keeping striped st st correct, cast off 2 sts at beg of next 2 rows. 23 (23: 25: 25: 27) sts.

Dec 1 st at each end of next and every foll alt row until 5 sts rem.

Work 1 row, ending with a WS row.

Left sleeve only

Next row (RS): K2tog, K1, cast off rem 2 sts.

Rejoin yarn to rem 2 sts with WS facing.

Right sleeve only

Cast off 2 sts at beg and dec 1 st at end of next row. 2 sts.

Both sleeves

Next row (WS): P2tog and fasten off.

MAKING UP

PRESS all pieces as described on the info page. Join raglan seams using back stitch, or mattress stitch if preferred.

Collar

With RS facing, 15mm (US 19) needles and yarn A, pick up and knit 7 (7: 7: 8: 8) sts up right side of neck, 4 sts from right sleeve, 10 (10: 10: 11: 11) from back, 4 sts from left sleeve, then 7 (7: 7: 8: 8) sts down left side of neck. 32 (32: 32: 35: 35) sts.

Row 1 (WS): K2, ★P1, K2, rep from ★ to end.

Row 2: K1, P1, ★K1, P2, rep from ★ to last 3 sts, K1, P1, K1.

Rep these 2 rows for 20 cm. Cast off in rib.

Insert zip into front opening, positioning top of zip 9 cm, above collar pick-up row. Fold collar in half to inside and slip stitch in place. See info page for finishing instructions.

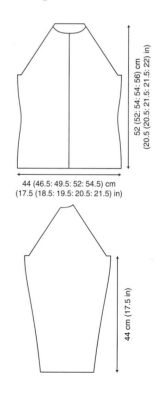

52 (52: 54: 54: 56) cm
(20.5 (20.5: 21.5: 21.5: 22) in)

44 (46.5: 49.5: 52: 54.5) cm
(17.5 (18.5: 19.5: 20.5: 21.5) in)

44 cm (17.5 in)

DESIGN NUMBER 8

MEG

KIM HARGREAVES

YARN

Rowan Big Wool

	XS	S	M	L	XL	
To fit bust	81	86	91	97	102	cm
	32	34	36	38	40	in
	5	5	6	6	7	x100gm

(photographed in Heaven 004)

NEEDLES

1 pair 15mm (US 19) needles

TENSION

7½ sts and 10 rows to 10 cm measured over reverse stocking stitch using 15mm (US 19) needles.

BACK

Cast on 29 (31: 33: 35: 37) sts using 15mm (US 19) needles.

Row 1 (RS): K0 (0: 0: 1: 0), P1 (2: 3: 3: 0), *K2, P3, rep from * to last 3 (4: 0: 1: 2) sts, K2 (2: 0: 1: 2), P1 (2: 0: 0: 0).

Row 2: P0 (0: 0: 1: 0), K1 (2: 3: 3: 0), *P2, K3, rep from * to last 3 (4: 0: 1: 2) sts, P2 (2: 0: 1: 2), K1 (2: 0: 0: 0).

Rep last 2 rows 3 times more.

Beg with a P row, cont in rev st st, inc 1 st at each end of 3rd and foll 8th row. 33 (35: 37: 39: 41) sts.

Cont straight until back measures 25 (26: 26: 27: 27) cm, ending with a WS row.

Shape armholes

Cast off 2 (2: 2: 2: 3) sts at beg of next 2 rows. 29 (31: 33: 35: 35) sts.

Dec 1 st at each end of next 2 (2: 3: 3: 3) rows. 25 (27: 27: 29: 29) sts.

Cont straight until armhole measures 22 (22: 23: 23: 24) cm, ending with a WS row.

Shape shoulders and back neck

Next row (RS): Cast off 3 sts, P until there are 6 (7: 7: 7: 7) sts on right needle and turn, leaving rem sts on a holder.

Work each side of neck separately.

Cast off 3 sts at beg of next row.

Cast off rem 3 (4: 4: 4: 4) sts.

With RS facing, rejoin yarn to rem sts, cast off centre 7 (7: 7: 9: 9) sts, P to end.

Work to match first side, reversing shapings.

FRONT

Work as given for back until 6 rows less have been worked to start of shoulder shaping, ending with a WS row.

Shape neck

Next row (RS): P9 (10: 10: 10: 10) and turn, leaving rem sts on a holder.

Work each side of neck separately.

Dec 1 st at neck edge on next 2 rows, then on foll alt row. 6 (7: 7: 7: 7) sts.

Work 1 row, ending with a WS row.

Shape shoulder

Cast off 3 sts at beg of next row.

Work 1 row. Cast off rem 3 (4: 4: 4: 4) sts.

With RS facing, rejoin yarn to rem sts, cast off centre 7 (7: 7: 9: 9) sts, P to end.

Work to match first side, reversing shapings.

SLEEVES (both alike)

Cast on 19 (19: 21: 21: 23) sts using 15mm (US 19) needles.

Row 1 (RS): P1 (1: 2: 2: 3), *K2, P3, rep from * to last 3 (3: 4: 4: 5) sts, K2, P1 (1: 2: 2: 3).

Row 2: K1 (1: 2: 2: 3), *P2, K3, rep from * to last 3 (3: 4: 4: 5) sts, P2, K1 (1: 2: 2: 3).

Rep last 2 rows 4 times more.

Beg with a P row, cont in rev st st, shaping sides by inc 1 st at each end of 3rd and every foll 8th row until there are 27 (27: 29: 29: 31) sts.

Cont straight until sleeve measures 44 (44: 45: 45: 45) cm, ending with a WS row.

Shape top

Cast off 2 (2: 2: 2: 3) sts at beg of next 2 rows. 23 (23: 25: 25: 25) sts.

Dec 1 st at each end of next and every foll 4th row until 17 (17: 19: 19: 19) sts rem, then on every foll alt row until 15 sts rem.

Dec 1 st at each end of next 3 rows, ending with a WS row. Cast off rem 9 sts.

MAKING UP

PRESS all pieces as described on the info page. Join right shoulder seam using back stitch, or mattress stitch if preferred.

Neckband

With RS facing and 15mm (US 19) needles, pick up and knit 8 sts down left side of neck, 7 (7: 7: 9: 9) sts from front, 8 sts up right side of neck, then 13 (13: 13: 16: 16) sts from back. 36 (36: 36: 41: 41) sts.

Row 1 (WS): K2, *P2, K3, rep from * to last 4 sts, P2, K2.

Row 2: P2, *K2, P3, rep from * to last 4 sts, K2, P2.

Rep these 2 rows for 10 cm. Cast off.

See information page for finishing instructions, setting in sleeves using the set-in method.

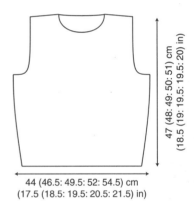

44 (46.5: 49.5: 52: 54.5) cm
(17.5 (18.5: 19.5: 20.5: 21.5) in)

47 (48: 49: 50: 51) cm
(18.5 (19: 19.5: 19.5: 20) in)

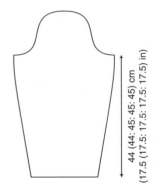

44 (44: 45: 45: 45) cm
(17.5 (17.5: 17.5: 17.5: 17.5) in)

LOLA

KIM HARGREAVES

YARN

Rowan Big Wool

	XS	S	M	L	XL	
To fit bust	81	86	91	97	102	cm
	32	34	36	38	40	in
	5	5	6	6	7	x100gm

(photographed in Smitten Kitten 003)

NEEDLES

1 pair 15mm (US 19) needles

TENSION

7½ sts and 10 rows to 10 cm measured over stocking stitch using 15mm (US 19) needles.

BACK

Cast on 31 (33: 35: 37: 39) sts using 15mm (US 19) needles.

Beg with a K row, work in st st as folls:

Work 4 (6: 6: 6: 6) rows, ending with a WS row.

Dec 1 st at each end of next and foll 6th row. 27 (29: 31: 33: 35) sts.

Work 5 rows, ending with a WS row.

Inc 1 st at each end of next and every foll 4th row until there are 33 (35: 37: 39: 41) sts.

Cont straight until back measures 31 (32: 32: 33: 33) cm, ending with a WS row.

Shape armholes

Cast off 2 (2: 2: 2: 3) sts at beg of next 2 rows. 29 (31: 33: 35: 35) sts.

Dec 1 st at each end of next 2 (2: 3: 3: 3) rows. 25 (27: 27: 29: 29) sts.

Cont straight until armhole measures 22 (22: 23: 23: 24) cm, ending with a WS row.

Shape shoulders and back neck

Next row (RS): Cast off 2 (3: 3: 3: 3) sts, K until there are 6 sts on right needle and turn, leaving rem sts on a holder.

Work each side of neck separately.

Cast off 3 sts at beg of next row.

Cast off rem 3 sts.

With RS facing, rejoin yarn to rem sts, cast off centre 9 (9: 9: 11: 11) sts, K to end.

Work to match first side, reversing shapings.

FRONT

Work as given for back until 6 rows less have been worked to start of shoulder shaping, ending with a WS row.

Shape neck

Next row (RS): K8 (9: 9: 9: 9) and turn, leaving rem sts on a holder.

Work each side of neck separately.

Dec 1 st at neck edge on next 2 rows, then on foll alt row. 5 (6: 6: 6: 6) sts.

Work 1 row, ending with a WS row.

Shape shoulder

Cast off 2 (3: 3: 3: 3) sts at beg of next row.

Work 1 row.

Cast off rem 3 sts.

With RS facing, rejoin yarn to rem sts, cast off centre 9 (9: 9: 11: 11) sts, K to end.

Work to match first side, reversing shapings.

SLEEVES (both alike)

Cast on 21 (21: 23: 23: 25) sts using 15mm (US 19) needles.

Beg with a K row, cont in st st, shaping sides by inc 1 st at each end of 13th and every foll 12th row until there are 27 (27: 29: 29: 31) sts.

Cont straight until sleeve measures 44 (44: 45: 45: 45) cm, ending with a WS row.

Shape top

Cast off 2 (2: 2: 2: 3) sts at beg of next 2 rows. 23 (23: 25: 25: 25) sts.

Dec 1 st at each end of next and every foll 4th row until 17 (17: 19: 19: 19) sts rem, then on every foll alt row until 15 sts rem.

Dec 1 st at each end of next 3 rows, ending with a WS row.

Cast off rem 9 sts.

MAKING UP

PRESS all pieces as described on the information page.

Join right shoulder seam using back stitch, or mattress stitch if preferred.

Collar

With RS facing and 15mm (US 19) needles, pick up and knit 8 sts down left side of neck, 9 (9: 9: 11: 11) sts from front, 8 sts up right side of neck, then 15 (15: 15: 18: 18) sts from back. 40 (40: 40: 45: 45) sts.

Beg with a P row, work in st st for 9 rows.

Next row: *K2, inc in next st, K2, rep from * to end. 48 (48: 48: 54: 54) sts.

Cont in st st until collar measures 22 cm from pick-up row.

Cast off.

See information page for finishing instructions, setting in sleeves using the set-in method and reversing collar seam for turn-back.

53 (54: 55: 56: 57) cm
(21 (21.5: 21.5: 22: 22.5) in)

44 (46.5: 49.5: 52: 54.5) cm
(17.5 (18.5: 19.5: 20.5: 21.5) in)

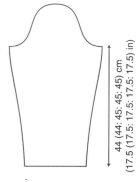

44 (44: 45: 45: 45) cm
(17.5 (17.5: 17.5: 17.5: 17.5) in)

Suzy

KIM HARGREAVES

YARN
Rowan Big Wool

	XS	S	M	L	XL	
To fit bust	81	86	91	97	102	cm
	32	34	36	38	40	in
		5	6	6	7	7	x100gm

(photographed in Shriek 005)

NEEDLES
1 pair 15mm (US 19) needles

BUTTONS – 5

TENSION
7½ sts and 10 rows to 10 cm measured over stocking stitch using 15mm (US 19) needles.

BACK
Cast on 31 (33: 35: 37: 39) sts using 15mm (US 19) needles.
Work in garter st for 6 rows, ending with a WS row.
Beg with a K row, cont in st st as folls:
Work 2 rows, ending with a WS row.
Dec 1 st at each end of next and foll 4th row.
27 (29: 31: 33: 35) sts.
Work 5 rows, ending with a WS row.

Inc 1 st at each end of next and every foll 4th row until there are 33 (35: 37: 39: 41) sts.
Cont straight until back measures 32 cm, ending with a WS row.
Shape raglan armholes
Cast off 2 sts at beg of next 2 rows.
29 (31: 33: 35: 37) sts.
Dec 1 st at each end of next 1 (3: 3: 3: 3) rows, then on every foll alt row until 9 (9: 9: 11: 11) sts rem.
Work 1 row, ending with a WS row. Cast off.

LEFT FRONT
Cast on 19 (20: 21: 22: 23) sts using 15mm (US 19) needles.
Work in garter st for 6 rows, ending with a WS row.
Next row (RS): Knit.
Next row: K4, P to end.
These 2 rows set the sts – front opening edge 4 sts worked in garter st with all other sts in st st.
Keeping sts correct, cont as folls:
Dec 1 st at beg of next and foll 4th row.
17 (18: 19: 20: 21) sts.
Work 5 rows, ending with a WS row.
Inc 1 st at beg of next and every foll 4th row until there are 20 (21: 22: 23: 24) sts.
Cont straight until left front matches back to beg of raglan armhole shaping, ending with a WS row.
Shape raglan armhole
Cast off 2 sts at beg of next row.
18 (19: 20: 21: 22) sts.
Work 1 row.
Dec 1 st at raglan armhole edge of next 1 (3: 3: 3: 3) rows, then on every foll alt row until 14 (14: 15: 16: 17) sts rem.
Work 1 row, ending with a WS row.
Shape front slope
Next row (RS): K2tog, K to last 4 sts and turn, leaving rem 4 sts on a holder. 9 (9: 10: 11: 12) sts.
Work 1 row.
Dec 1 st at each end of next and every foll alt row until 1 (1: 2: 1: 2) sts rem.
Medium and extra large sizes
Dec 1 st at raglan armhole edge only on foll alt row. 1 st.
All sizes
Next row (WS): P1 and fasten off.
Mark positions for 5 buttons along left front opening edge – first to come level with 9th row, last to come just below start of front slope shaping and rem 3 buttons evenly spaced between.

RIGHT FRONT
Cast on 19 (20: 21: 22: 23) sts using 15mm (US 19) needles.
Work in garter st for 6 rows, ending with a WS row.
Next row (RS): Knit.
Next row: P to last 4 sts, K4.
These 2 rows set the sts – front opening edge 4 sts worked in garter st with all other sts in st st.
Keeping sts correct, cont as folls:
Next row (RS): K1, K2tog, yfwd (to make first buttonhole), K to last 2 sts, K2tog (for side seam dec).
Working a further 4 buttonholes in this way to correspond with positions marked on left front for buttons, complete to match left front, reversing shapings.

SLEEVES
Cast on 19 (19: 21: 21: 23) sts using 15mm (US 19) needles.
Work in garter st for 6 rows, ending with a WS row.
Beg with a K row, cont in st st, shaping sides by inc 1 st at each end of 5th and foll 10th row, then on every foll 8th row until there are 27 (27: 29: 29: 31) sts.
Cont straight until sleeve measures 44 (44: 45: 45: 45) cm, ending with a WS row.
Shape raglan
Cast off 2 sts at beg of next 2 rows.
23 (23: 25: 25: 27) sts.
Dec 1 st at each end of next and every foll alt row until 5 sts rem.
Work 1 row, ending with a WS row.
Left sleeve only
Next row (RS): K2tog, K1, cast off rem 2 sts.
Rejoin yarn to rem 2 sts with WS facing.
Right sleeve only
Cast off 2 sts at beg and dec 1 st at end of next row. 2 sts.
Both sleeves
Next row (WS): P2tog and fasten off.

MAKING UP
PRESS all pieces as described on the information page.
Join raglan seams using back stitch, or mattress stitch if preferred.
Left collar
Slip 4 sts left on left front holder onto 15mm (US 19) needles and rejoin yarn with RS facing.

Cont in garter st as folls:

Work 1 row, ending with a RS row.

Inc 1 st at end of next and every foll alt row until there are 12 sts.

Cont straight until collar, **unstretched**, fits up left front slope, across top of left sleeve and across to centre back neck.

Cast off.

Right collar

Slip 4 sts left on right front holder onto 15mm (US 19) needles and rejoin yarn with WS facing.

Cont in garter st as folls:

Work 1 row, ending with a WS row.

Inc 1 st at end of next and every foll alt row until there are 12 sts.

Cont straight until collar, **unstretched**, fits up right front slope, across top of right sleeve and across to centre back neck.

Cast off.

Join centre back seam of collar, then sew shaped edge of collar to neck edge. See information page for finishing instructions.

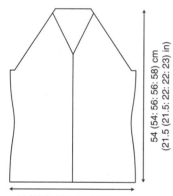

44 (46.5: 49.5: 52: 54.5) cm
(17.5 (18.5: 19.5: 20.5: 21.5) in)

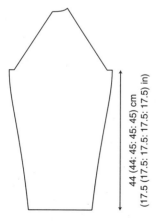

MAY

KIM HARGREAVES

YARN

Rowan Big Wool   1   x   100gm
(photographed in Sherbet Lime 002)

NEEDLES

1 pair 15mm (US 19) needles

TENSION

7½ sts and 10 rows to 10 cm measured over stocking stitch using 15mm (US 19) needles.

FINISHED SIZE

Completed hat measures approx 53 cm (21 in) around head.

HAT

Cast on 40 sts using 15mm (US 19) needles

Beg with a K row, work in st st as folls:

Work 16 rows, ending with a WS row.

Shape crown

Row 1 (RS): (K7, K3tog) 4 times. 32 sts.

Work 1 row.

Row 3: (K5, K3tog) 4 times. 24 sts.

Work 1 row.

Row 5: (K3, K3tog) 4 times. 16 sts.

Work 1 row.

Continued on page 22.

DEE DEE

KIM HARGREAVES

YARN

Rowan Big Wool

A   White Hot 001   1   x   100gm

B   Black   008   1   x   100gm

(also photographed in A – Sherbet Lime 002 and B – Smitten Kitten 003)

NEEDLES

1 pair 15mm (US 19) needles

TENSION

7½ sts and 10 rows to 10 cm measured over stocking stitch using 15mm (US 19) needles.

FINISHED SIZE

Completed scarf is approx 20 cm (8 in) wide and 200 cm (79 in) long.

SCARF

Cast on 15 sts using 15mm (US 19) needles and yarn A.

Row 1 (RS): Using yarn A knit.

Row 2: Using yarn A K2, P11, K2.

Rows 3 to 14: As rows 1 and 2.

Break off yarn A and join in yarn B.

Rows 15 to 28: As rows 1 and 2 but using yarn B.

Continued on page 22.

BILLIE

KIM HARGREAVES

YARN

Rowan Big Wool

	XS	S	M	L	XL	
To fit bust	81	86	91	97	102	cm
	32	34	36	38	40	in
	3	3	4	4	4	x100gm

(photographed in Sherbet Lime 002)

NEEDLES

1 pair 15mm (US 19) needles

TENSION

7½ sts and 10 rows to 10 cm measured over stocking stitch using 15mm (US 19) needles.

BACK

Cast on 28 (30: 32: 34: 36) sts using 15mm (US 19) needles.
Beg with a K row, cont in st st as folls:
Work 4 rows, ending with a WS row.
Dec 1 st at each end of next and foll 4th row.
24 (26: 28: 30: 32) sts.
Work 3 (5: 5: 5: 5) rows, ending with a WS row.
Inc 1 st at each end of next and every foll 6th row until there are 30 (32: 34: 36: 38) sts.
Cont straight until back measures 28 (29: 29: 30: 30) cm, ending with a WS row.

Shape armholes

Cast off 2 (2: 2: 2: 3) sts at beg of next 2 rows.
26 (28: 30: 32: 32) sts.
Dec 1 st at each end of next 2 (2: 3: 3: 3) rows.
22 (24: 24: 26: 26) sts.
Cont straight until armhole measures 20 (20: 21: 21: 22) cm, ending with a WS row.

Shape shoulders and back neck

Next row (RS): Cast off 2 (3: 3: 3: 3) sts, K until there are 4 sts on right needle and turn, leaving rem sts on a holder.
Work each side of neck separately.
Cast off 2 sts at beg of next row.
Cast off rem 2 sts.
With RS facing, rejoin yarn to rem sts, cast off centre 10 (10: 10: 12: 12) sts, K to end.
Work to match first side, reversing shapings.

FRONT

Work as given for back until 6 rows less have been worked to start of shoulder shaping, ending with a WS row.

Shape neck

Next row (RS): K7 (8: 8: 8: 8) and turn, leaving rem sts on a holder.
Work each side of neck separately.
Dec 1 st at neck edge on next 2 rows, then on foll alt row. 4 (5: 5: 5: 5) sts.
Work 1 row, ending with a WS row.

Shape shoulder

Cast off 2 (3: 3: 3: 3) sts at beg of next row.
Work 1 row.
Cast off rem 2 sts.
With RS facing, rejoin yarn to rem sts, cast off centre 8 (8: 8: 10: 10) sts, K to end.
Work to match first side, reversing shapings.

MAKING UP

PRESS all pieces as described on the information page.
Join right shoulder seam using back stitch, or mattress stitch if preferred.

Collar

With RS facing and 15mm (US 19) needles, pick up and knit 7 sts down left side of neck, 8 (8: 8: 10: 10) sts from front, 7 sts up right side of neck, then 15 (15: 15: 17: 17) sts from back.
37 (37: 37: 41: 41) sts.
Row 1 (WS): K1, *P1, K1, rep from * to end.
Row 2: P1, *K1, P1, rep from * to end.
Rep last 2 rows 4 times more.

Row 11: Inc in first st, *P1, inc in next st, rep from * to end. 56 (56: 56: 62: 62) sts.
Row 12: K2, *P1, K2, rep from * to end.
Row 13: P2, *K1, P2, rep from * to end.
Rep rows 12 and 13 until collar measures 20 cm from pick-up row.
Cast off in patt.
See information page for finishing instructions, reversing collar seam for turn-back.

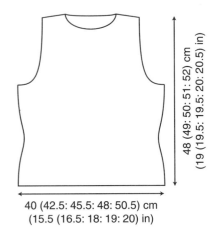

48 (49: 50: 51: 52) cm
(19 (19.5: 19.5: 20: 20.5) in)

40 (42.5: 45.5: 48: 50.5) cm
(15.5 (16.5: 18: 19: 20) in)

May

Continued from page 21.
Row 7: (K1, K3tog) 4 times. 8 sts.
Work 1 row.
Break yarn and thread through rem 8 sts. Pull up tight and fasten off securely.

MAKING UP

PRESS as described on the information page.
Join back seam, reversing seam for roll.

Dee Dee

Continued from page 21.
Break off yarn B and join in yarn A.
Rep last 28 rows until scarf measures approx 200 cm, ending after 14 rows using yarn B.
Cast off.

MAKING UP

PRESS as described on the information page.

INFORMATION PAGE

TENSION

Obtaining the correct tension is perhaps the single factor which can make the difference between a successful garment and a disastrous one. It controls both the shape and size of an article, so any variation, however slight, can distort the finished look of the garment.

We recommend that you knit a square in pattern and/or stocking stitch (depending on the pattern instructions) of perhaps 5 - 10 more stitches and 5 - 10 more rows than those given in the tension note. Press the finished square under a damp cloth and mark out the central 10cm square with pins. If you have too many stitches to 10cm try again using thicker needles, if you have too few stitches to 10cm try again using finer needles. Once you have achieved the correct tension your garment will be knitted to the measurements indicated in the size diagram shown at the end of the pattern.

SIZING AND SIZE DIAGRAM NOTE

The instructions are given for the smallest size. Where they vary, work the figures in brackets for the larger sizes. **One set of figures refers to all sizes**.

Included with every pattern in this magazine is a 'size diagram', or sketch of the finished garment and its dimensions. The purpose of this is to enable you to accurately achieve a perfect fitting garment without the need for worry during knitting. The size diagram shows the finished width of the garment at the under-arm point, and it is this measurement that the knitter should choose first; a useful tip is to measure one of your own garments which is a comfortable fit. Having chosen a size based on width, look at the corresponding length for that size; if you are not happy with the total length which we recommend, adjust your own garment before beginning your armhole shaping - any adjustment after this point will mean that your sleeve will not fit into your garment easily - don't forget to take your adjustment into account if there is any side seam shaping. Finally, look at the sleeve length; the size diagram shows the finished sleeve

measurement, taking into account any top-arm insertion length. Measure your body between the centre of your neck and your wrist, this measurement should correspond to half the garment width plus the sleeve length. Again, your sleeve length may be adjusted, but remember to take into consideration your sleeve increases if you do adjust the length - you must increase more frequently than the pattern states to shorten your sleeve, less frequently to lengthen it.

CHART NOTE

Many of the patterns in the book are worked from charts. Each square on a chart represents a stitch and each line of squares a row of knitting. Each colour used is given a different symbol or letter and these are shown in the **materials** section, or in the **key** alongside the chart of each pattern.

When working from the charts, read odd rows (K) from right to left and even rows (P) from left to right, unless otherwise stated.

KNITTING WITH COLOUR

There are two main methods of working colour into a knitted fabric: **Intarsia** and **Fairisle** techniques. The first method produces a single thickness of fabric and is usually used where a colour is only required in a particular area of a row and does not form a repeating pattern across the row, as in the fairisle technique.

Intarsia: Cut short lengths of yarn for each motif or block of colour used in a row. Joining in the various colours at the appropriate point on the row, link one colour to the next by twisting them around each other where they meet on the wrong side to avoid gaps.

Fairisle type knitting: When two or three colours are worked repeatedly across a row, strand the yarn **not** in use loosely behind the stitches being worked. It is advisable not to carry the stranded or "floating" yarns over more than three stitches at a time, but to weave them under and over the colour you are working. The "floating" yarns are therefore caught at the back of the work.

FINISHING INSTRUCTIONS

After working for hours knitting a garment, it seems a great pity that many garments are spoiled because such little care is taken in the pressing and finishing process. Follow the following tips for a truly professional-looking garment.

PRESSING

Darn in all ends neatly along the selvage edge or a colour join, as appropriate.

Block out each piece of knitting using pins and gently press each piece, omitting the ribs, using a warm iron over a damp cloth. **Tip**: Take special care to press the edges, as this will make sewing up both easier and neater.

STITCHING

When stitching the pieces together, remember to match areas of colour and texture very carefully where they meet.

Use a seam stitch such as back stitch or mattress stitch for all main knitting seams, and join all ribs and neckband with a flat seam unless otherwise stated.

CONSTRUCTION

Having completed the pattern instructions, join left shoulder and neckband seams as detailed above.

Sew the top of the sleeve to the body of the garment using the method detailed in the pattern, referring to the appropriate guide:

Square set-in sleeves: Set sleeve head into armhole, the straight sides at top of sleeve to form a neat right-angle to cast-off sts at armhole on back and front.

Shallow set-in sleeves: Join cast-off sts at beg of armhole shaping to cast-off sts at start of sleeve-head shaping. Sew sleeve head into armhole, easing in shapings.

Set-in sleeves: Set in sleeve, easing sleeve head into armhole.

Continued overleaf

Continued from previous page

JOIN SIDE AND SLEEVE SEAMS.

Slip stitch pocket edgings and linings into place.

Sew on buttons to correspond with buttonholes.

After sewing up, press seams and hems.

Ribbed welts and neckbands and any areas of garter stitch should not be pressed.

ABBREVIATIONS

K	knit
P	purl
st(s)	stitch(es)
inc	increas(e)(ing)
dec	decreas(e)(ing)
st st	stocking stitch (1 row K, 1 row P)
garter st	garter stitch (K every row)
beg	begin(ning)
foll	following
rem	remain(ing)
rev	revers(e)(ing)
rep	repeat
alt	alternate
cont	continue
patt	pattern
tog	together
mm	millimetres
cm	centimetres
in(s)	inch(es)
RS	right side
WS	wrong side
sl1	slip one stitch
psso	pass slipped stitch over
p2sso	pass 2 slipped stitches over
tbl	through back of loop
M1	make one stitch by picking up horizontal loop before next stitch and knitting into back of it
yfwd	yarn forward
yrn	yarn round needle
yon	yarn over needle
cn	cable needle

EXPERIENCE RATINGS

= Easy, straight forward knitting

= Suitable for the average knitter

= For the more experienced knitter

STOCKIST INFORMATION

ROWAN OVERSEAS DISTRIBUTORS

BELGIUM
Pavan
Koningin Astridlaan 78
B9000 Gent
Tel: (32) 9 221 8591

CANADA
Diamond Yarn
9697 St Laurent
Montreal
Quebec
H3L 2N1
Tel: (514) 388 6188
www.diamondyarns.com

Diamond Yarn (Toronto)
155 Martin Ross
Unit 3
Toronto
Ontario
M3J 2L9
Tel: (416) 736 6111
www.diamondyarns.com

DENMARK
Individual stockists
- please contact Rowan for details

FRANCE
Elle Tricot
8 Rue du Coq
67000 Strasbourg
Tel: (33) 3 88 23 03 13
www.elletricote.com

GERMANY
Wolle & Design
Wolfshovener Strasse 76
52428 Julich-Stetternich
Tel : (49) 2461 54735.
www.wolleundesign.de

HOLLAND
de Afstap
Oude Leliestraat 12
1015 AW Amsterdam
Tel : (31) 20 6231445

HONG KONG
East Unity Co Ltd
Room 902,
Block A
Kailey Industrial Centre
12 Fung Yip Street
Chai Wan
Tel : (852) 2869 7110.

ICELAND
Storkurinn
Kjorgardi
Laugavegi 59
Reykjavik
Tel: (354) 551 82 58

JAPAN
DiaKeito Co Ltd
2-3-11 Senba-Higashi
Minoh City
Osaka
Tel : (81) 727 27 6604
www.rowanintl-jp.com

NORWAY
Hera
Tennisun 3D
0777 OSLO
Tel: (47) 22 49 54 65

SWEDEN
 Wincent
Norrtulsgaten 65
11345 Stockholm
Tel: (46) 8 673 70 60

U.S.A.
Rowan USA
5 Northern Boulevard
Amherst
New Hampshire 03031
Tel: (1 603) 886 5041/5043

For details of U.K. stockists or any other information concerning this book please contact:
Rowan Yarns, Green Lane Mill, Holmfirth, West Yorkshire HD9 2DX
Tel: +44 (0)1484 681881   Fax: +44 (0)1484 687920
Email: seasons@knitrowan.com www.knitrowan.com

Cat

Meg

Lola

Jerry

Chrissie

Suzy